Contents

Fiction

Non Fiction

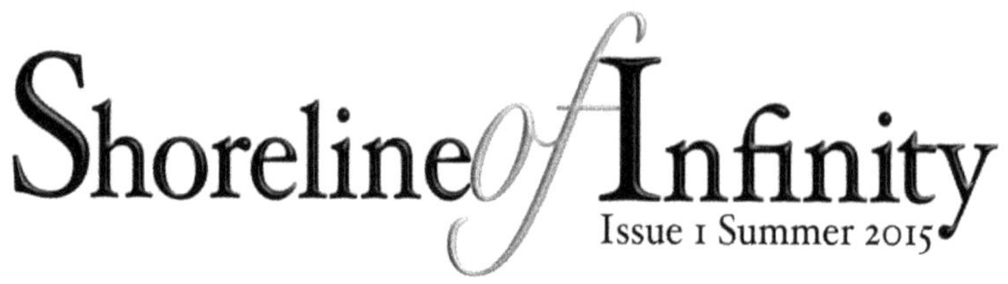

Science Fiction Magazine from Scotland

ISSN 2059-2590
ISBN 2370000266811

Publisher
The New Curiosity Shop
8 Craiglockhart Bank
Edinburgh
EH14 1JH
Scotland

web: www.shorelineofinfinity.com
email: contact@ShorelineofInfinity.com
twitter: @shoreinf

Editor-in-Chief: Noel Chidwick
Art Director: Mark Toner
Assistant Editor: Russell Jones

Subscriptions to *Shoreline of Infinity* are available. Visit the website for details.
Shoreline of Infinity is available as an ebook or in print.
Submissions of fiction, art, reviews, non-fiction are welcome:
contact the editor via the website.

Cover image: Bill Wright

v25915i

Pull up a Log

Come, pull up a log, sit down, warm your extremities by our fire. You've travelled a long way, friend, and you have a long journey ahead. Have we got some stories for you. Our story tellers have travelled a long way too. This is Larry, and he's got a heartwarming tale of old Japan. Alex there takes us to a distant moon. Colleen—hi Colleen—her story is a little thriller of a piece. Richmond warns you not to muck about with a time machine—you didn't come via a time machine, did you? Joseph's and Guy's stories give reality a tweak on the nose while Claire and David, well they take us somewhere else. M Luke McDonnell's story asks if we really know what's going on inside our partner's mind. That old cove over there? That's John Buchan: he's got a science fiction story he's been wanting to re-tell for a long while. Yes you're right—John is the one who wrote The Thirty Nine Steps.

We've also been joined by Charles Stross, to tell us a little bit about his own writing and his thoughts on science fiction. He reminds us that SF isn't about naively predicting the future: it's about figuring out what human beings will make of the future. And here's Steve. He's sat round many a fire like this over the years, engaging folk with his thoughts. He's revisiting a Glasgow SF Convention and talking about two films produced 23 years apart. And we can recommend some books to take with you as you journey on.

Mark has also gathered a fine team of artists to join us and they have captured the essence of each story.

These fine folk are why Mark and I decided to set up *Shoreline of Infinity*: we wanted somewhere to come to read tales with a twist, fables to explore our uncertain future. Of all the fictions, SF is the one of ideas and possibilities, but just as importantly it's about how we humans can cope—or otherwise—in a world so intense we are pressured into packing our thoughts into 140 letters. The human race has come a long way and we're at a point now where we should stop, look around, think about where we are and where we want to go before moving on. As Charles Stross also says, one of the functions of fiction is play, to learn how to manage in life.

Science Fiction is a beach where we can build sandcastles of futures and alternative realities, and here at the Shoreline of Infinity, we have plenty of sand.

One day, maybe you'll tell us your story?

Noel Chidwick, Editor-in-Chief, Shoreline of Infinity.
Edinburgh
June 2015

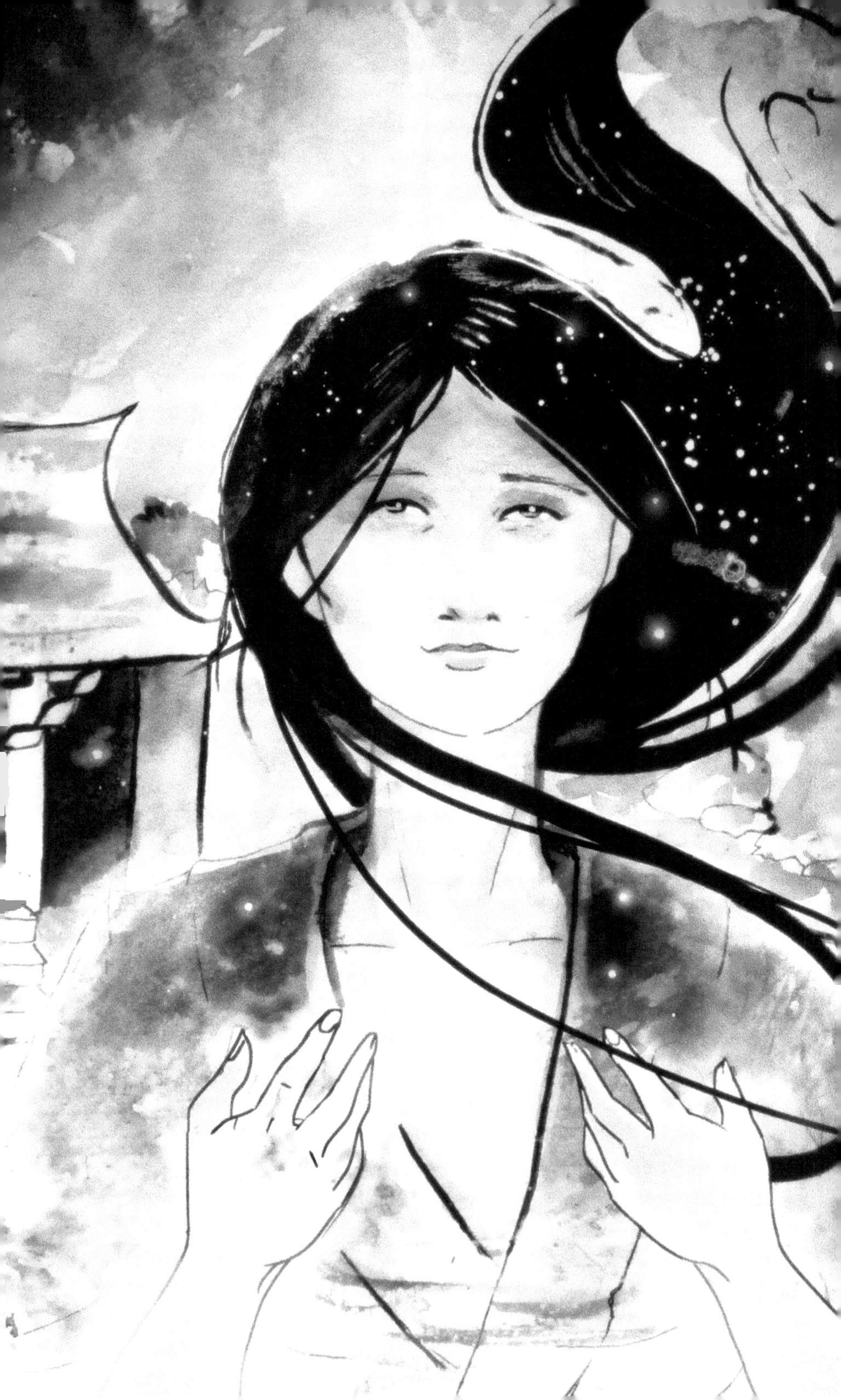

The Three Stages of Atsushi

Larry Ivkovich

Sagami Province, Japan
Muromachi period, 1531 CE

Dressed in a faded and tattered mourning kimono, Michiko appeared wrapped as if in a darkened shroud as she knelt before the *hokora* shrine. For a moment Atsushi hesitated as he walked toward her, a chill running up his back. *Is this my wife?* he thought. *Or some fallen kami?*

A warm breeze carried the faint odor of incense as well as Michiko's whispered words to Atsushi as he shook himself free of the unease he felt. "Great Amaterasu, Ruler of the Plain of Heaven, hear my plea," Michiko murmured, her eyes closed, her head bowed, her hands clasped in her lap. On the small wooden shrine's stone base, the candles' flames wavered in that errant wind. Once again Atsushi had awakened to find Michiko had stolen away in the dawn's light to make her futile entreaties to the sun goddess.

It was a beautiful, clear morning with the sunrise casting a dazzling light over his and Michiko's small farm and its surrounding acreage. The flower gardens Michiko tended were full of warm, bright colors and fragrances. The surface of the Sakawa river glittered on the flat horizon like dancing jewels. Such calmness belied the raging waters of last spring season which had overflowed the Sakawa's banks to wreak great destruction on all around it.

Atsushi's rice crop was just beginning to come back a year after the flood; the remaining fruit trees showed their first signs of blossoming. With the help of his neighbors and their bakafu landowner, he had rebuilt his small wooden house and, he had hoped, his and Michiko's lives as well. But it was not to be, it seemed. He stopped a few feet from Michiko who appeared oblivious to his presence, lost in her endless grief and despair.

"Michiko," he said, his fists clenched at his side as he fought the storm of emotions warring within him. "Please come away from there."

"Amaterasu, I beg you, let my son be saved," Michiko continued as if not hearing him. "Let me bring him back from Death's dominion. I will offer you anything of myself in return."

"Michiko." Atsushi's patience had grown thin since the death of their son. That terrible loss had been hard but he had moved on with life, as empty and troubled as it seemed at times. Michiko had not. He reached down, grasped his wife gently under her thin arms and pulled her to her feet.

Michiko's graying hair was tied in a topknot for her morning ritual; the white face-paint she had applied to her once-beautiful features streaked with tears. She blinked rapidly as if waking from a deep sleep. She had lost weight from not eating much and, as such, was as light as a grass doll.

"Atsushi?" she said, looking at him as if seeing him for the first time. Michiko shook her head, her gaunt features etched with anguish. "I could have saved him," she said, her voice breaking. "Osamu would be here today if I had acted more swiftly."

"And you would be dead too," Atsushi interrupted softly, pulling her to him in a tight embrace. How many times must he reassure her before she would believe him? "The flood waters would have borne you away with him, never to return. Osamu is dead. You must stop this."

As Michiko began to sob against his shoulder, as her frail body shook uncontrollably, Atsushi struggled against his own tears. Amaterasu! Always Amaterasu, the false goddess, and this terrible guilt Michiko felt! Michiko had lost a son, it was true, but he had lost Osamu too and it felt like he was now losing his wife. Slowly and as surely as the sun shone in the sky, Michiko was slipping away from him.

Such cruelty in the world, he thought angrily, not for the first time. *Do the gods or the kami even care?* As he led Michiko into the house, it was then he remembered...

It is flying, father! Flying!"

Atsushi laughed in delight at the sight of his son. Osamu ran across the small field behind their house, towing a high-flying kite in his excited wake. The "paper hawk" was one Atsushi had purchased on his last trip to Odawara, spending a great deal of his hard-earned money to buy it.

Despite Michiko's admonitions about such an exorbitant sum, it had been worth the price to see the joy on Osamu's face. It was his son's seventh birthday today, after all, and what better way to celebrate as well as honor the gods to ensure a good harvest for the coming year?

The kite was shaped like a bird of fire, as long and wide as Osamu was tall. It darted through the cloudless blue sky as if alive swooping and soaring, twisting and climbing. As the wind finally died and the kite fell spiraling to earth, Atsushi joined his son.

"Honorable Father," Osamu said as he reeled in the kite's string tether. "If it please you to listen, I have an idea."

"Ah," Atsushi said, feigning great seriousness. Osamu sometimes acted more like an adult than a child. "What would that be?"

Osamu stood over his kite, his small brows furrowed in thought, his brown eyes narrowed. His dark hair had been mussed by the wind. His short pants were grass-stained from where he had fallen running after his kite.

"I have heard stories of Chinese soldiers borne aloft by giant kites," his son finally said. "Perhaps Hojo Ujitsuna could do the same with his *samurai*. They could surprise their enemies from above."

War and battle again. His son rarely talked of anything else these days. Yet, since Soun Ujitsuna of the Hojo Clan ruled nearby Odawara and protected the surrounding countryside, it seemed a harmless enough preoccupation. Michiko was wrong to worry so about it. Like all things childish, Osamu would soon grow out of it. Atsushi himself once had such aspirations—to attain a respectable position in life, to become someone of modest wealth and benevolent power. But that was long ago, another lifetime. He knelt down beside Osamu. "Interesting. But they would have to be very big and strong kites."

Osamu nodded. "But it could be done, yes?"

"Perhaps. But, as everything else in life, such an undertaking would have to be done in well-planned stages. The kites must be designed, then built and tested, then the soldiers trained in their use, and, finally, a great strategy devised for the attack. It would not be accomplished in one quick step."

Osamu considered that for a moment and said, "Then I will think on that more carefully for I am sure it can be done. And then, with your permission, Honorable Father, I will notify Hojo Ujitsuna. And perhaps he will take it to the Shogun and to the Emperor of the Jade Court himself!"

Atsushi suppressed a smile. His son could be so serious and imaginative! Surely, those were traits he had inherited from Michiko. "Very well," he said, employing his most important tone of voice. "I am certain you will come up with a solution. Now, come, your mother has prepared a delicious supper for us."

Such a precious memory, Atsushi thought as he walked the rice paddies that afternoon. *But that is all Osamu is now: a shadow from the past.*

At that moment, a group of samurai rode over the crest of the hill. It was not unusual to see the armed warriors. In these never-ending days of constant fighting among the feudal *daimyo*, such soldiers often passed on the road near his farm traveling to or from Odawara—they had done so periodically for the last two years. Aatsushi's *bakafu* landowner had an agreement with the samurai and certain warlords, which thankfully kept the war at a distance.

As a result, Atsushi had become friendly with one or two of the samurai. As had his son, Osamu, before the flood. Osamu had been greatly interested in the samurai and all manners of weaponry, much to Michiko's dismay.

But, as these four rode closer, two mounted on horseback in front and two in back of an attendant-borne palanquin, Atsushi realized he did not recognize them. Plus, they were fronted by a trio of brightly costumed musicians, beating drums and ringing bells.

Eerily, the sun clouded over as if setting a stage for some dramatic *Noh* play. Atsushi realized also the birds had stopped singing; the sounds of insects were no longer apparent. It was as if the creatures of the natural world had vanished.

Alarmed at such a foreboding coincidence, he quickly looked toward the flower gardens where Michiko knelt among the maiden lilies—she was intent on what she was doing and had not looked up. Thankfully, the gardens still held her interest after Osamu had died. Even her talent for creating *origami* birds and animals had faded since the flood. At least gardening kept her somewhat occupied. But before Atsushi could tell Michiko to go inside the house, one of the samurai hailed him.

As the warrior directed his mount closer, Atsushi wiped his hands on his trousers, removed his hat and bowed. "Good day, honored Lord," he said. "How may a humble farmer assist you?"

The samurai stopped a few feet from Atsushi, looking down on him. The soldier was in full armor and struck an impressive and frightening pose. The stylized metal mask he wore, hiding the warrior's features, chilled Atsushi to his core with its stark otherworldliness. A *kitana* and *wakizashi* hung in belted scabbards at his side, the long and short swords of the warrior class intimidating even when sheathed.

The samurai's armor, unlike the other soldiers Atsushi had encountered, looked new and untouched by battle. And there were faint colors swirling in its surface as if the reflections of a rainbow flickered there. His answer to Atsushi's question was surprising and unexpected. "My master wishes to speak to your wife."

Atsushi blinked. "My wife?" He again looked toward Michiko who stood and stared at the palanquin. She held some weeds she had pulled in one hand; the simple shirt and trousers she wore were smeared with dirt. Her hair had loosened enough to allow some long, stray strands to hang limply.

The passenger in the conveyance had risen from his seat, also standing and returning his wife's gaze. He was tall, thin and very pale, garbed in a long, belted, dark robe, his long white hair tied behind his back. His fingernails were painted black.

"Honored Lord," Atsushi began but when he turned back to the samurai, the armored warrior had wheeled his horse around and was returning to his position behind the palanquin.

"Michiko..." But Atsushi found himself rooted to the spot, suddenly unable to move. His legs felt heavy, his feet like giant stones. His voice faltered as he watched Michiko walk toward the black-robed man.

There the two spoke in hushed tones, the man nodding and smiling, Michiko with head bowed and shoulders hunched. He held something out to Michiko who took it and clasped it to her breast. With a pale hand, the man drew some sign in the air between the two of them, bowed, and climbed back into his palanquin.

As if obeying some unspoken command, the four servants picked the palanquin up and, with the samurai and musicians, continued on down the road.

Atsushi could move again. "Michiko!" he cried, stumbling toward the road. "What did that man want? What is it he gave you?"

His wife looked at him then, her features aglow, a smile widening on her face. Atsushi stopped, startled. He hadn't seen Michiko smile in a very long time. By that simple act, she had become beautiful once more. His heart leapt at the sight.

In her hands, she held a small scroll. "He is a *majo*, a servant of Amaterasu, and has instructed me how to save Osamu." And with that announcement, Michiko strode back to the house, her head held high and the smile remaining.

No, no! Atsushi started running. He would catch up with this majo, this witch, and make him pay for deceiving his wife! How dare he take advantage and give her such false hope! Samurai or not, he would punish them for their disrespect.

But they were gone. Atsushi stopped, his mouth agape. The road ran straight and true for miles beyond his farmhouse toward Odawara. The group of samurai and the palanquin they escorted would not have gotten far; he should have seen them clearly. Yet, there was nothing; the road lay empty of life.

The sun came out from behind whatever cloud had hidden it. In the distance, a catbird trilled.

✣

Atsushi remembered the flood as if it were yesterday. He had been so determined to stay. He thought they would be safe. Why had he been so stupidly proud and stubborn? Look what it had cost him.

He sat at the wooden table in their house, a bowl of boiled cabbage and noodles sitting untouched in front of him, a bottle of *shochu* standing half empty. From his and Michiko's sleeping room, he could hear his wife reciting verses. She had drawn the curtain and had been reading from the majo's scroll into the early evening. He could make no sense of those parts he heard.

He sat slumped in his chair, staring into space, his head bobbing with the numbing effects of the shochu. He didn't have the strength to confront his wife anymore, almost as if the majo had placed a spell over him as well. I have failed, he thought. I have failed to help my family. My son is dead and my wife is mad. What have I done to deserve this? What god or kami have I offended?

"It was my fault," he mumbled drunkenly. "Not Michiko's. Osamu-san, Michiko-san, forgive me, my son, my wife. Forgive me." He put his head down on the table and began to weep. And, slowly, his eyes began to close as he drifted into a troubled sleep...

...and woke to the sound of singing.

What is this? Atsushi raised his head, trying to shake the sleep from his clouded mind. His mouth was dry, his head was pounding, his stomach roiled sourly from the shochu.

The voice intoned again, clearly, distinctly. He knew that sound though he hadn't heard its loveliness in such a very long time. Michiko was outside, singing.

He stumbled into the cool air of early morning. He had slept all night! Squinting into the bright sunlight he saw his wife. Once again Michiko attended their household hokora shrine, giving clear, lilting intonation to a song Atsushi didn't recognize. She stood with her arms crossed at her breast, dressed in the same clothes she had worn in the garden yesterday, her feet bare, her hair hanging loosely about her shoulders.

"Michiko!" he cried. "What are you doing?"

Michiko began to glow. Atsushi stopped and looked away. A trick of the light! He was still half-asleep, still suffering from having drunk too much shochu. By all that was sacred, surely he was dreaming.

He looked back and fell to his knees, heart hammering in his chest. A shimmering blue radiance surrounded his wife, making her appear like some *kami* from the Invisible World. Her hair writhed serpent-like around and above her head as if alive. Her clothes clung to her as if blown by a great wind. Michiko held her hands out to him. "Atsushi-san," she said, smiling. "Beloved husband. Do not fear for me. I am going back to save Osamu. And you must remember what has happened here. Look for my paper dragon! With the majo's help I have placed it where you will only find it when the time is right. Do you hear? We will all be together again, I know it!"

Her paper dragon? What was she saying to him? "Michiko! Michiko!"

Like an earthbound star, the light erupted into an explosion of blue lambency. Michiko vanished within that azure cocoon, shafts of fiery radiance spreading outward like grasping tendrils. Atsushi cried out and covered his eyes.

Atsushi rose slowly to his feet from where he knelt at Michiko's grave. Once again he had placed some maiden lilies at the burial site. They had been her favorite flowers and fitting for one so brave and selfless and he had tried his best to keep them growing. It was one way of remembering her, of honoring her. Michiko had given her life to save Osamu from last year's flood. Atsushi was nothing compared to her, she of the courageous heart. She had always hated war and killing and yet, in the end, displayed more courage and selflessness than an entire army of samurai.

Osamu. Blinking back tears, Atsushi made his way toward his house. He must see to his son.

Ever since Michiko had died in the fierce waters of the swollen Sakawa the year before, Osamu had never been the same. Only seven years old, he had been the light of Atsushi's and Michiko's lives. Full of energy and humor, mature and wise beyond his years, now the boy ate and spoke little and slept most days, crying for his mother.

As Atsushi stepped into his house, a momentary reverie came over him. He leaned against the entryway, feeling suddenly drowsy and weak. For a moment, a vision appeared to him—Michiko surrounded in blue light, a smile upon her face.

He shook his head, the sobbing of Osamu breaking the strange trance. What magic was this? Was he losing his mind? Did he even care anymore? With a shrug, he stepped into his son's small sleeping room. There, Osamu lay, crying and mumbling in his sleep. Atsushi knelt down on the straw *tatami* mat and placed his hand on his son's forehead.

Hot, so hot. Fevered, delirious. The flood still ravaged their lives so long after it had come and gone! *What can I do?* Atsushi thought, hanging his head. *Pray? There is no one or nothing to pray to! The gods have deserted us if they ever existed at all.*

It was then he saw the paper dragon. It lay on the floor near the foot of the mat. Atsushi stared. It looked like the cranes and other birds and animals Michiko used to make. He hadn't seen this one before. How had it gotten here? Slowly he reached down and picked up the *origami* creature and through some urging not his own, as if another's hand guided him, he carefully unfolded it.

There was writing within. Atsushi stared at the small chop mark printed on one side of the paper. It wasn't familiar to him, but the script that flowed beneath it, so crisp and elegant, was Michiko's.

With shaking hands, Atsushi started to read. "Dearest Atsushi-san," the missive began. "I hope you and Osamu are well. If you are reading this, then that is because I no longer exist in the realm of the living. But I also do not abide in the afterlife but somewhere between, awaiting the next stage of our journey."

He paused, holding his breath. Reluctantly, as if beckoned, he looked again at the letter. It *was* written in Michiko's hand. Once more, he read.

"Have you remembered yet what happened? The majo explained it all to me. Those higher goals we seek must be reached in stages; nothing can happen overnight or with one simple act. Even the building of a house occurs in many steps. You, yourself, have always believed thusly. I have heard you recite this to Osamu many times and so do the gods themselves work their wonders—one step at a time.

"So I have gone to complete the second stage of this journey, Osamu's death being the first, and you must now complete the third and final one. It is the only way that you and I and Osamu can be a family again. We could not do this together but only separately, as painful as that is. That is why neither the majo nor I told you before. It was not yet your turn.

"Heed what I say, my love. Osamu was not to be taken by the flood; he has to grow up to fulfill a great destiny and you and I must be there to aid him in achieving that. He will help to end this terrible conflict among the *daimyos* and restore peace to our land. You must remember, Atsushi. For all of our sakes, remember."

Rage exploded within Atsushi. He ran outside, screaming at the sky above, giving voice to all the pain and frustration that had built up inside of him.

"Michiko! Michiko!" he cried, shaking his fists at a passing cloud. "What does it mean? What are you trying to tell me?"

Madness! Madness! And yet... Atsushi sat down on the soft grass, suddenly weak and dizzy. It was happening again—in his mind's eye, he saw his wife enveloped in a blazing blue light, returning to rescue Osamu from the flood, to sacrifice herself to save their son.

Could it be? Memories rushed back, cascading through his thoughts like the rampaging waters of the Sakawa. He lowered his head into his hands, gasping at the intensity of the images filling his mind.

Yes, yes. He *did* remember! By all that was sacred, what Michiko's spectral message told of was true!

The third and final stage—Atsushi must now do the same to save all three of them as Michiko had done to save Osamu. Could he really do it? Could he? "Amaterasu," he whispered, reaching out despite his disbelief. "Help me."

A dull grayness enveloped the landscape as the sun vanished behind a gathering of thunderheads. Atsushi stood in the quiet, hearing only a beating of drums and a ringing of bells. He quickly walked to the road where, just at the crest of the hill, a procession of samurai, musicians, and a palanquin being borne by four attendants appeared, the palanquin's occupant a white-maned man garbed in a black robe.

Just like the first time.

I know this, he thought, breathing quickly. *I have seen this before. And now I must do what needs to be done.* Joyous laughter bubbling in his throat, his spirit soaring, Atsushi ran to meet the majo.

The heavens above Sagami province shone a brilliant blue. Small, fluffy clouds scudded here and there, adding their feathery shapes to a glorious morning sky. Birds flitted from tree to ground and back again. Insects buzzed and the sun warmed the very air itself, shining shafts of golden light everywhere.

Atsushi and Michiko stood in the doorway of their house, watching Osamu at play. "The wooden sword you made for him is being put to good use, it seems," Michiko said with a playful smile. "He is pushing back the enemy attack."

Atsushi laughed, admiring his wife's beauty and pleased at her witty remark. He thanked the gods and the *kami* every day for her! "Perhaps he will become a samurai," he said.

Michiko's face darkened. "I pray not but who knows what the gods have in store for us? The terrible wars continue and remember the flood of last year. If not for you, we would have all perished."

"How can I forget? But we have survived both, have we not?" Atsushi glanced away then. Something tickled at the back of his mind, some memory trying to surface, some image of the past that lurked there and then, just as abruptly, was gone.

He said softly and slowly, the reason for the words a mystery, "It may be that Osamu will grow up to help bring peace to all of us." He turned to see Michiko staring at him strangely.

"Perhaps," she said with a nod, a faraway look in her eyes. "Perhaps. That would be a good thing, yes?"

Atsushi nodded as he and Michiko clasped hands and turned back to look with pride upon their son.

Larry Ivkovich's genre work has been published in over twenty online and print magazines. He has been a finalist in the L. Ron Hubbard's Writers of the Future contest and was the 2010 recipient of the CZP/Rannu Fund award for fiction. Published novels include urban fantasy The Sixth Precept (IFWG Publishing), and fantasy Blood of the Daxas (Assent Publishing).
Larry lives in Pennsylvania, US

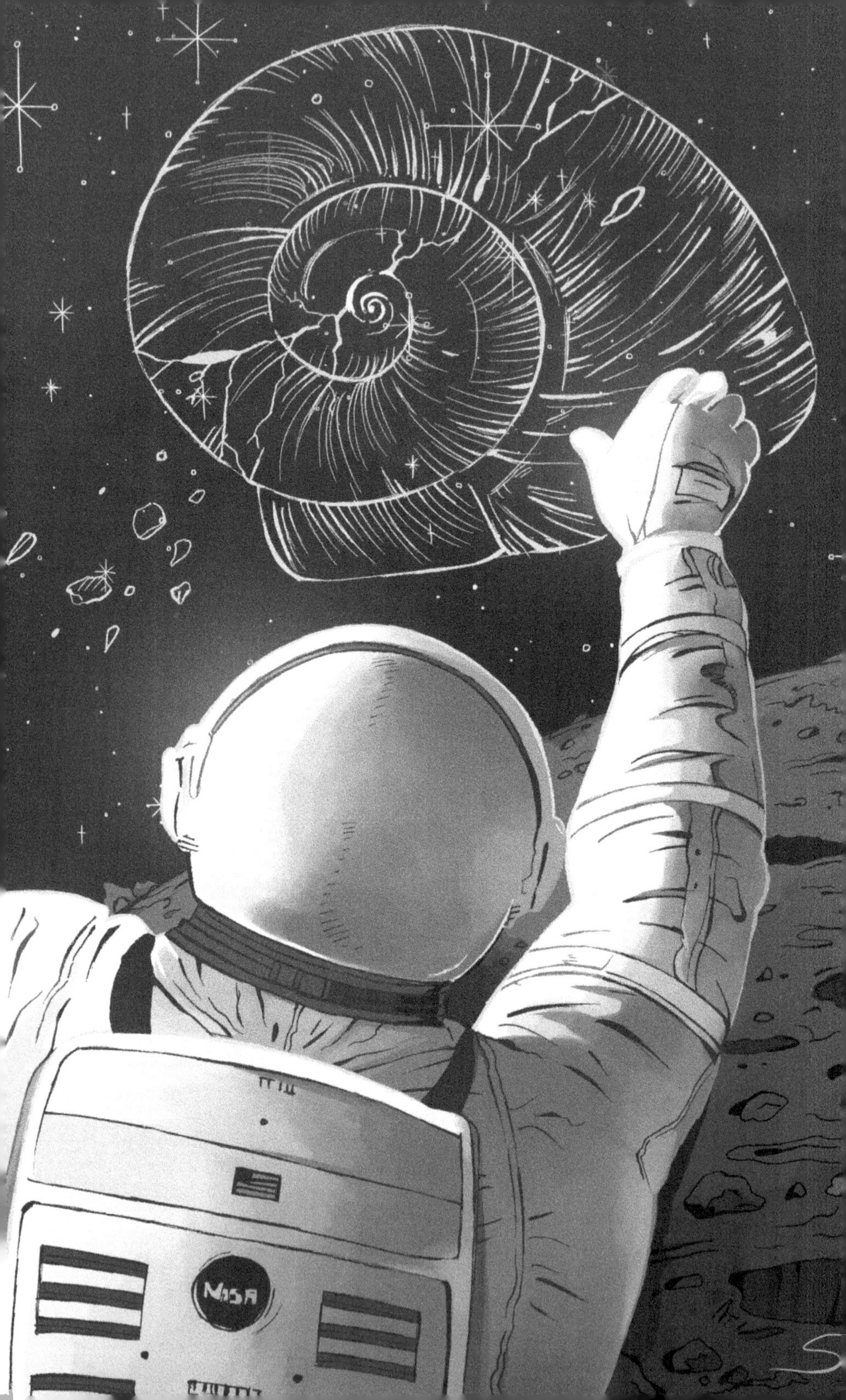
NASA

The Spiral Moon

Alex Barr

I'm off on a world tour before I die. This little world is mine alone now. I'm leaving Ernesto, with his leprous head, stiff as a statue. I'll know when I've been right round because he'll be sitting there.

It's good to be moving. And to feel calm. It has to end? It has to end. And, oh! The stars! Collecting samples I was too busy bending, but now there's no point I can look up. Sirius is just above the horizon like the world's biggest diamond. Not twinkling of course, just . . . there.

The horizon is less than a hundred metres away. Earth should rise over it soon, between Perseus and Auriga. It was so clear from the cabin window, blue and white, oh yes. As my world sweeps towards Jupiter, Earth will shrink to a star, with no-one here to see. Ah, there's Rigel! And off to the right, the Milky Way, like a necklace of—

Aah!

Falling. No, floating like in a dream. Off a big escarpment. A crater in fact. Thirty metres deep, at a guess, and a half mile across. Now I've reached the floor. Rocky hummocks like country loaves. But I'm not hungry, ha ha. Rigel and Sirius have gone below the rim. I'm travelling quite fast now. It's like being on an invisible bike. Hey, think of a name for this crater. When you find this recording, folks, remember Letitia saw it first.

Climbing out. Phew. Harder than I thought despite tiny gravity. Sweating already. Soon I'll see Sirus again and . . . Oh God. Oh God, no. Visor misting. I'm losing the stars!

I'm scared. I'm alone. For a moment I forgot what's coming. Sorry folks, I'll be all right. Well, I won't be, but still . . . I'm sitting on a rock, resting. Mum, Dad, Elsa, Earl, Anna, love you all. Not forgetting Mark. Yes you, Mark, no hard feelings. Don't any of you be sad, I had my adventure. Who could have thought a small meteoroid would end it?

There must have been a scattering of them, like bird shot. And suddenly our bird was dead. Escaping oxygen froze to a cloud of pearls. Beautiful. Sad wires like severed nerves. Natasha would have died instantly from decompression. No sense of horror—more like a movie, or breaking down in the car waiting for recovery.

Over the intercom the collision nearly cracked my eardrums. Guess it's left me with tinnitus because now there's a swishing, like the sea in a seashell. Communication was routed through the crew capsule, so I'm cut off. But help would arrive too late anyway. Oh well, you're all here in my head, Mum, Dad, Elsa, Earl, Anna, Mark, so Letitia's not alone . . . but my head will end up like Ernesto's, and where will you all be then?

Ernesto couldn't wait. Sat on a rock, waved, made a throat-cutting gesture, unsnapped his helmet and took it off. It drifted down slowly, turning, sun glinting on the visor. His dark skin turned white, like a line of subzero washing. His black hair turned to grey wool. His sample bag is beside him. Does it hold the iron, nickel, or platinum he hoped for?

I've left my own samples near him. If they show signs of living organisms I'll never know. What a joke—I come looking for life, and the looking ends my life. And is knowing whether life came from space going to solve the Earth's problems? Anyway, didn't life on Earth begin in rock pools? Where are the rock pools here?

But hey, if I have found traces of organisms I'll be famous, a twenty-first century Darwin. Ha ha. What a price for posthumous fame! Does Shakespeare know he's a phenomenon? Does he wallow in his success? No-one there to wallow. And what about all my memories? Sunrise from a mountain ridge. That night on the little island with Mark—the smell of our campfire, the smell of your skin against mine. Being picked for this mission, desert sun through the minibus windows on the way to the first briefing. I'm labelling boxes no-one else can open.

But here's one I want to open for all of you. You never knew why I changed. Complained that I was driven, full of my new direction, no time for any of you. You didn't know failure was what drove me, a very public failure, though even you Anna, dear Anna, in the audience, never knew the full story.

Ravel's *Daphnis et Chloé*. Act One nearly over, the prima ballerina slips and pulls a muscle. As company physio I lay her out in the green room and massage her wonderful thighs.

She sobs, "Will I get back on, Letitia?"

"Hope so."

"I must. That cow Amelia, my understudy—she'll be rubbing her hands."

"Well I'm rubbing your legs, Carmen, so let's hope."

She makes a gesture of despair, so elegant you'd think despair was beautiful, like excavated bones.

"What the hell did I slip on? Had nobody swept the stage? What time is it?"

"Ten minutes to Act Two. Try standing."

A few steps, then a few pliés.

"I can't go on!"

"Lie down. Let's not give up."

In comes an ASM. "This must be what threw you, Carmen."

An opal earring, the tiny rock that ended my first career. And a big rock has ended my second. Oh I must see the stars! Turn up my heating to warm the visor. The batteries will run down fast and shorten my life, but a life without stars . . .

Carmen moans, "Who dropped it? That toe-rag Amelia? Let her take over. Let them see what a clunker she is."

"Turn over." And after a few minutes, "Stand."

She stands. "Not sure, Letitia."

"You'll be fine."

"Honestly?" On her points, testing.

"Carmen, honestly. Carry on."

Five minutes into Act Two, airy grace is reduced to a heap of limbs. I rush on and rub her thighs in desperation.

She hisses, "You sad useless bitch."

The lights blot out the audience, but tier upon tier of eyes watch my downfall.

When we trained for this mission we thought the more we talked about death the less likely it was. I remember laughing, "I've died already. On stage."

I can see the stars again! So clear I could almost reach out and touch them. The tiniest are like flour on a slate worktop. Ah, breadmaking . . . Yes, Mark, never forgave me, did you? Thought I should have married you instead of earning my PhD in astrobiology. Lived with you and made babies instead of doing astronaut training. But I thought when I came back to Earth there'd be time for that. And here I am, no bread, no babies. Driven by curiosity. Another dead cat.

I'm moving on, watching my feet because if I trip and smash my visor I'll be dead, ha ha, but also watching the sky. There's Rigel again, and Orion's belt. The M42 Nebula in his sword is like brightly lit gauze in a theatre set. Betelgeuse, a brilliant red. The Milky Way over to the right. Lynx spread out further over. Oh, there's Capella in Auriga. I want to seize those million stars for myself. Pour them into a magic bucket and clamp the lid on. No, no, that's ridiculous. Stay there, stars! You're just the jewels in my Granddad's watch, the eyes of sheep in a field at night, the sparkle on waves.

The terrain is fairly even now, so I can bounce along quite—oh God. It's Ernesto. Am I all the way round already? But how did I miss seeing Earth? Oh. Now I'm close I can see. Just another rock. A rock you could mistake for a frozen man. Oh stop it Letitia, EVA suits aren't designed to cry in. Can't wipe my eyes, damn it. I'm hugging this rock anyway. Leaning on it like I leaned on so many summit rocks on Earth's wonderful mountains, gazing at other mountains, or at mist. I'm in sunlight again, it's throwing my long shadow on the ground, sharp, the shape of the helmet somehow monstrous. Stage lighting—but no audience.

Moving again. Goodbye Ernesto-not-Ernesto. Is Mehmet still alive I wonder? Folks, please contact his family and explain what happened. The Agency will, but I'd like you to as well. When the rock struck, the mooring line tore loose and the crew capsule drifted off. Ballet in slow motion. Mehmet must have thought Natasha survived and could be rescued. He pressed down on his camera tripod and used it as a vaulting pole. Up, up, up he went, because escape velocity here is next to nothing.

He scraped along the side of our doomed craft, but couldn't get a hold and floated past. I watched him shrink, only his sunlit side visible, the shadow side merging with the blackness, half of him gone already. How will he cope in that void? At least I have my world tour. He once told me, "Nothing in the universe is not Allah, nothing not Allah is in the universe." Comforting, Mehmet? Using up your oxygen with Sufi chanting? Bless you.

A little further and I'll rest.

I see Earth! At last. A perfect opal laid on black silk. There, white sea-thrift will be stirring in the breeze. Drifts of bluebells will be a sapphire Milky Way. My parents will inherit my notebooks with sketches of seabirds—and Mark. Soaked from a sudden downpour we took refuge in a ruined barn. Pressed our bodies together and slowly Mark, with fingers like a blind man's, unbuttoned my shirt . . .

The sun is high now. Harsh light, no dappled shade. On Earth are the woods where I walked beside rushing water. My little dog Sally panting in my tracks. Woods and water! None here. She thrust her nose into piles of dead leaves and scattered them. That ancient smell like no other. Sometimes the path veered off up the steep valley side. We didn't want to leave the river. Sally kept stopping to look into it, whether she recognized her reflection I don't know. But when we pushed ahead the brambles became too dense, and poor Sally was like the ram caught in a thicket. So up we went, and it was like my career, forced away from what I loved but ending higher.

Science. I'll die for science. Of what, I wonder. Cold, when the batteries fail? Oxygen deprivation? Asphyxiation when the canisters in my backpack stop absorbing CO2? Why have I never thought about people who wait to die? Túpac Amaro the Second in the plaza in Cuzco, when they roped his wrists and ankles to four horses, and he waited to hear the whips that would drive them to tear him apart? How did resistance fighters feel, in total dark in a basement waiting for the Gestapo? I will face this waiting, I will. I mean to know every moment, to the last.

Four years to this asteroid's next approach to Earth. Will you find this recording then? If so, here's how I'd like my funeral. Forget after-life, and that soppy stuff saying I'm the wind rustling the leaves. Say I never reached the big four-oh, which saved me feeling depressed about it. I'd like Mark to come, and if he doesn't shed a tear I'll haunt him. I'd like some everything's-OK music. George Winston playing Pachelbel's Canon?

Oh Anna, when you lost Sammy I stayed away. Couldn't face your suffering. Tried to write but couldn't think of anything real. Now I would know what to write. That crater I fell in—I name it after you. Maybe at my funeral you could read 'Ulysses' by Tennyson (yes I know it's about exploring in old age). Or anything to say the world is fine without Letitia.

I'm cold. Can't remember where I said I'm going. I seem to be in a ravine. Am I supposed to name these features? The Valley of the Shadow? It must be late—the sun has gone and the stars are out. I think the others are expecting me. Ernesto is quite a character. When he retires he's going to teach skydiving. New Mexico or somewhere. Natasha's lovely. She wants to raise a big family. And Mehmet is going to create a garden. He says a garden is a mirror of paradise.

Here it's very bare. No trees. And I can't walk properly. I just float, it's quite distressing. But I must press on before bedtime. Keep going, Let—whatever your name is. Oh, this landscape. How to describe it? Strained. No, that's not the word, strange is the word. Shallow ridges, like the beach at . . . Oh come on, Daddy, you remember the one. When I was down and angry just after I left the ballet? I didn't confess my failure, and you didn't press me. We walked dodging waves, you talked about shells. You called mussels bivalves of the subclass *pteriomorphia*. You said spiral shells grow around a columella. I felt the poetry of science. When you showed me the spiral moon shell I knew I'd found my calling.

You said, "A beach is the only place in the universe where solid, liquid, and gas coexist." I can hear the sea in my earphones, Daddy, but it seems to have gone right out. I'm scared. Freezing cold. Who am I and where do I belong? Anna, that monk who taught you meditation sends loving kindness everywhere. Everywhere, you said. Does it reach me?

These ridges. Long slanting shadows. Keep . . . what's the word? Going. Keep going, Let—whoever. Don't get your boots wedged in the gaps. No Daddy, I won't.

Ernesto's coming! At last. Walking towards me with that what-the-hell macho stride, arms out like a gunfighter. Waving hello. Hello, Ernesto! If I didn't have this weird thing in front of my face I'd kiss you. And here's Mehmet showing me his garden. Beautiful peach colored tulips and purple roses. How did they grow so fast?

I hope he won't think I'm rude but first I have to greet Mummy and Daddy. Hello! Hello! Oh, and Elsa and Earl are with them. And Anna. Oh, Anna! And who's that in the distance? Surely not Mark? It is! What are they doing? They seem to be chanting, and Daddy's leading them. It's the names of shells. I'll join in.

Lu-na-tia her-os
north-ern moon snail
Tcct-ari-us pa-go-das
pa-go-da prick-ly win-kle
My-tilis e-du-lis
blue mus-sel
Ne-ve-rita he-li-coi-des
lovely lovely *spi-ral m . . . m . . . m . . .*

Alex Barr's latest publication is *Take a Look at Me-e-e!* a book of stories for children (Pont Books 2014). He came second in the Willesden Herald story competition 2011. His stories have been on Radio 4. His maths was too weak for astronomy (his first love) but fine for architecture.

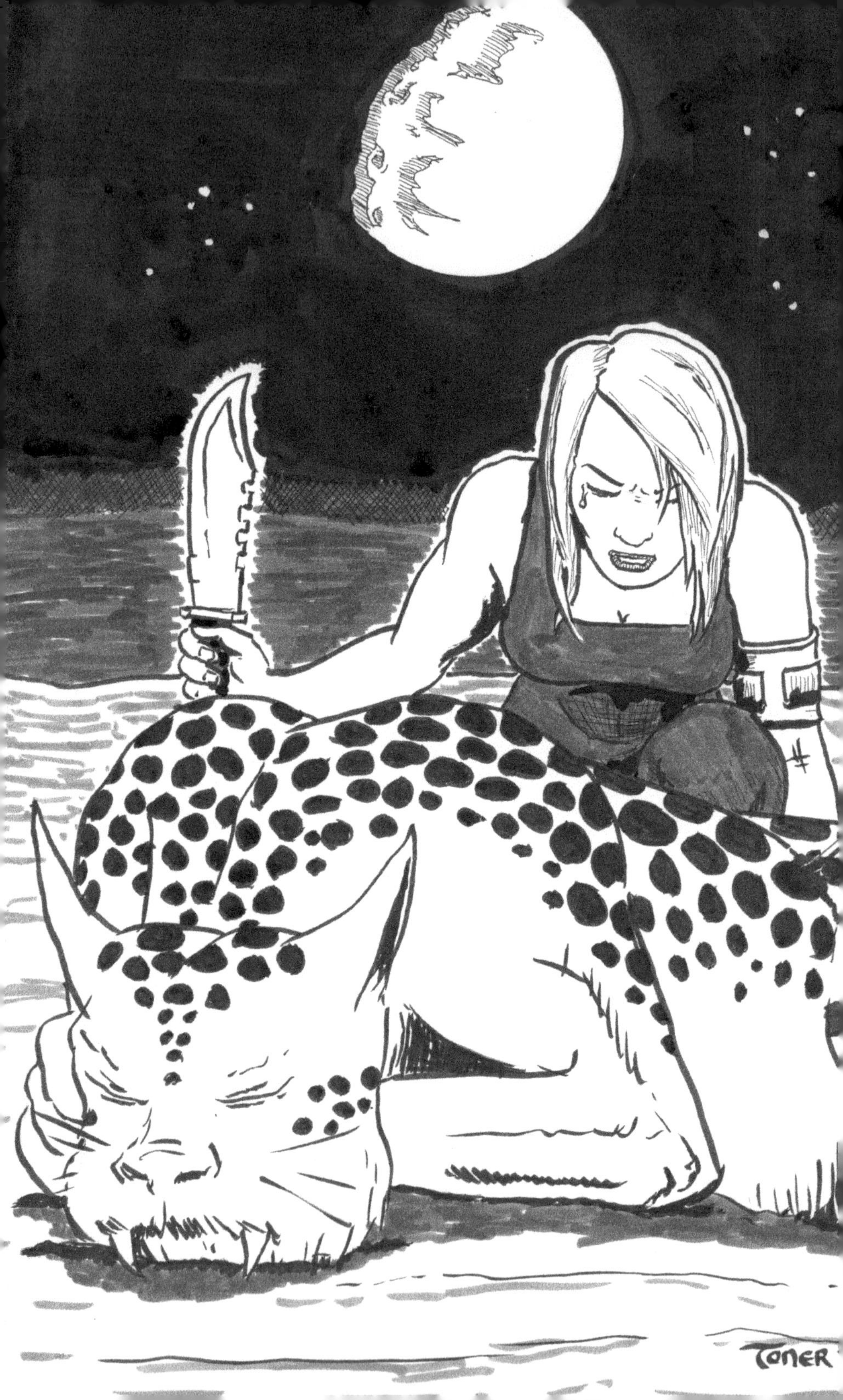
TONER

Symbiosis

Colleen Anderson

The acrid cloying blood, the wet pulling apart of skin and muscle sluicing about her feet made her gorge rise. Keela swallowed reflexively, trying to rid herself of bitter saliva as blood clotted the sand beneath her in the still night air.

She threw the pelt onto the sand, wiping sweat from her eyes, not to mention the tears forming hotter trails over her cheeks. Hateful work. Why couldn't the gods have sent something deserving of being killed? Why something so beautiful, yet terrifyingly efficient as a force of nature? They all had to survive, though, even the great cats, but Keela did not know if she could continue much more fighting, fearing, being a monster. Yet, weren't they all? Leaden exhaustion weighted her limbs and mind.

Keela tucked the serrated knife in its sheath and folded the skin into the pack, then strapped it to her back. It would serve as a sunbreak for Yasmeen as she healed…if she healed. Then Keela looked up at the boat of the gibbous moon, wishing it would carry her back to those first months when this had seemed just a small pastoral planet, teeming with nothing larger than the beaver-sized herbivores. Now, there were only twenty researchers left and three years to wait until the next supply ship. Their equipment had died first, prey to the vagaries of electromagnetic fluctuations and heavy metals. This howling wasteland of a parched planet was slowly eating them. The heat, the lack of water, the giant black and white spotted cats, canines curving down like a sabertooth's, all of it, tried to expel the people for the invading bodies they were.

When Yasmeen had been attacked by this cat, Keela had shot an arrow that wounded it, then tracked it, to fight a deadly winner-takes-all. She checked the suture patch over her arm, making sure blood was not leaking through. The night painted the blood a sinister substance and it spotted her skin as if she were a great cat too. Loading meat into the second pack, Keela then took bearings, hoping they could come back for more, should it prove edible.

She began trudging back to the base camp, searching for the one remaining white dome. It was clear how much they stood apart from this apparently simple planet. Everything flowed, sinuous, moving from one state or space with apparent ease. Wind undulated the sand into rippling dunes. Short grasses moved in waves. What sparse trees there were curved branches back toward the earth, as if afraid to bear the full brunt of the harsh white sun. The cats and the herbivores all seemed to flow, as if embodying the properties of the rare sightings of water.

Keela listened to the odd pops and snaps that filled the night air. She turned slowly as she walked, trying to gauge the landscape for movement, her eyes straining against the pale light. Cocking her head, she sniffed, feeling the taint of heat. Morning would soon be ripping away the evening. Muttering, "I want to live, I want to live," Keela tramped determinably until the low rumble of the cats permeated her chant.

Another slow pirouette revealed three slinking shapes. That was it then; she would become part of the ecosystem by joining the food chain. She would fight. No…no use. There was no hope with three. A frozen silhouette, against the night's backdrop, she thought quickly, madly, not wanting to die.

Maybe, maybe there was one way to survive.

Carefully she eased the pack off that held the meat, then the other. Crouching slowly onto all fours, she pulled out the glossy black and white pelt, and threw it over her shoulders and head. Gritting her teeth against the disgusting dank feel, she hunkered under the sticking, stinking hide. She hoped they would ignore her, think her a dead cat. Scratches and cuts stung where the dead skin touched her. She clutched the knife, a pitiful defense against the curving scythes of the great cats' claws.

The gruesome clamminess was still preferable to feeling fangs sink into her flesh. Tears leaked from her eyes as the throaty huffs sounded closer. Gagging beneath the pelt, she felt her suture patch give way and the weight of the skin settle firmer against her. Something stepped on her—the great head-sized pad of the cat—and crushed her into sand and darkness.

Weight pushed onto her, squeezed the air out and all she could smell was cat and dirt and blood. She stifled her nausea. Not moving, breathing slowly, shallowly, she let the spotted coat blanket her, completely conceal her in its gummy funeral gloom. She waited as one with it, believing she was nothing more. The great cats must believe that it was one of their own that had died.

Pain knifed through her, rippling in a spasm. They weren't attacking but one of her cuts might be infected. Still, she remained stationary as the cats moved off and the pain took her breath away, sealing blackness beneath her eyelids.

Heat filled her. A hot breath. She rose, sloughing off the beast and stared at the other three. Her whiskers twitched as she swung her great head about. This was how she survived, flowing with the planet's ways. A growl escaped her throat as she cursed the heavens, and loped off to the caves.

Colleen Anderson's 200 plus pieces of fiction and poetry are in such venues as *Chilling Tales, Evolve, Exile Book of New Canadian Noir* and *Cemetery Dance*. She has been an Aurora nominee, and is in *Imaginarium* and *Best of Horror Library*. New pieces are coming in *Nameless, Our World of Horror, OnSpec, Black Treacle*, and *Pantheon*.

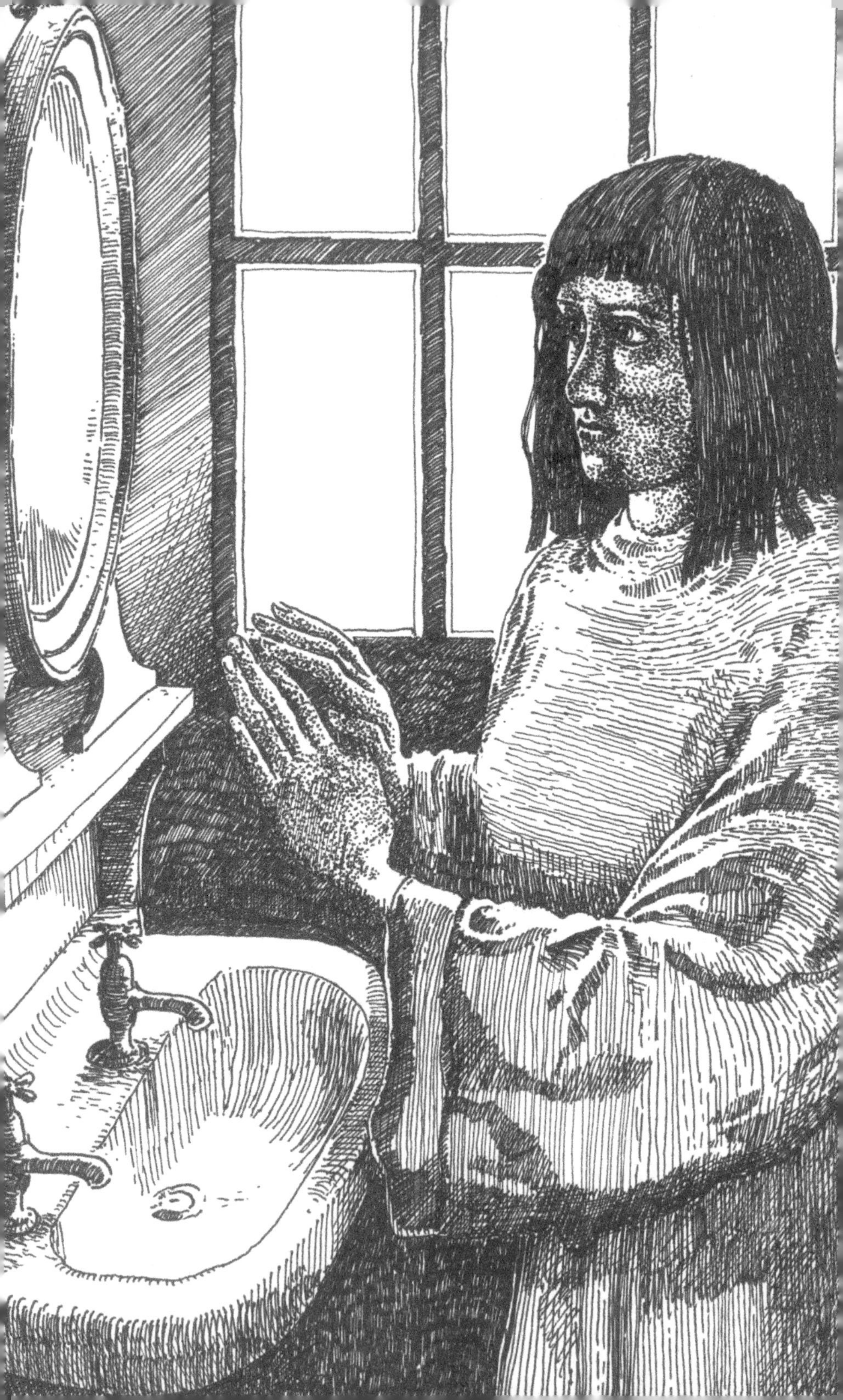

See You Later

M Luke McDonell

Arabella's front door beeped in polite disapproval of her polymer-coated iris. Hurriedly, she typed in the long access code and held her palm to the scanner, but too late. Mrs. Constantino was out of her apartment and shuffling down the hall towards her, the frayed hems of her oversized sweat pants dragging on the clean white carpet.

"Something wrong, honey? Lock stuck? I've been having the same trouble with my windows. I called the management company but all they do is send a reset code that doesn't fix anything."

Arabella breathed through her mouth to avoid the smells of vodka and cat pee that blanketed the old woman. All the residents complained that they'd moved into this building to get away from the riffraff on the streets and now they had to deal with it in the halls. Mrs. Constantino was somehow able to afford the sky-high rent though, so there was nothing to be done about her.

The lock retracted but Arabella held the door shut. Mrs. Constantino was oblivious to polite hints and would stay for hours if she let her in.

"You okay, honey? You been crying?" Mrs. Constantino asked.

Arabella resisted the urge to rub her aching eyes. The technician warned her not to touch them for 24 hours. "No, I just got AR lenses."

Mrs. Constantino's wrinkled face lit up in a smile. "You're going to love them. I can see better than a hawk now."

Arabella forced herself to examine Mrs. Constantino's bloodshot eyes and indeed, a thin silver line traced the iris. Where *did* this woman get her money? "I didn't need them for medical reasons," she admitted. "I have 20/10 vision now."

Mrs. Constantino winked. "You don't have to tell me these are more than fancy glasses."

As she drew in a burbling breath to elaborate, Arabella pushed the door open and slipped inside. "I'm supposed to rest," she called in weak apology as she slammed the door behind her.

In the bathroom, she stared at the silver ring of her iris with distaste. The irony was that Hugh hadn't wanted the lenses either. He treated his body like a rare sports car, too precious to drive. When his company insisted that all senior management get the permanent implants – a bleeding-edge technology not yet legal in the EU – he actually considered quitting.

Arabella rarely put her foot down but in this case she did so with force. Her husband's last promotion was contingent on a move to this decrepit city – one of the last outposts of cheap labor. She'd had to leave her friends, her favorite sushi restaurant, and the hairdresser she'd finally trained to give her a proper cut. Hugh would damn well get some plastic in his eye after all the sacrifices she'd made.

She'd grown to regret her insistence. Hugh had become increasingly distant in the months since he'd gotten the implants. He came home from work earlier, but shushed her when she tried to speak to him.

"I'm in a meeting," he'd say, exasperated, waving his hand to indicate a conference table she couldn't see. He moved through the apartment in strange patterns, avoiding things that weren't there and clipping the edges of furniture that was.

He wouldn't watch streams with her on the wall anymore, declaring the resolution inferior to what his eye screens displayed. In theory, they could view the same content simultaneously and Hugh made a show of synching his glasses with the wall, but when he sat next to her, head tilted to the ceiling, giggling during the tense parts of dramas, she knew he was seeing something else.

They'd had plenty of bumps on the road of marriage before, but at least they'd been looking out the same windshield. She would fix this.

Arabella ran icy cold water over her face until the pain in her eyes subsided. She had to hurry. Hugh would be home from work soon. He didn't know she was getting lenses, so hadn't bothered to lock the settings he'd spent months perfecting.

She approached the strange contraption in his office hesitantly. The black goggles, mounted on a thick silver pole, resembled a grotesque Venetian *carnevale* mask, wires instead of ribbons trailing from both edges. The technician had explained that the tiny screens needed to be recharged once a day and that was a good time to adjust settings as well. Contrast, brightness, automatic data overlays – Arabella had only half-listened to the detailed instructions. She'd use Hugh's settings; that was the point of getting these, after all.

She leaned in. Tiny white words appeared in the darkness. *Recharge?* in the center, *Yes* and *No*, on the far left and right respectively, appeared beneath.

Arabella gazed steadily at *Yes*.

A green circle appeared. Watch the dot for the next 15 seconds. Please do not blink, the text directed.

So far, so good. After the elapsed time, another menu appeared. *Update settings?* And beneath, *Home, Work,* and *New.*

She selected *Home* and held still as information was transferred to the tiny processors.

Your update is complete.

Arabella straightened, blinking rapidly in the suddenly too-bright light. What was this? The view from the upper-floor window was no longer of polluted Lake Tanganyika but of a busy, beachfront promenade. Bikini-clad teen girls, pale, sweaty tourists, and overly-tanned men in linen suits paraded past a backdrop of white sand and turquoise sea.

It took her a moment to recognize this was Ocean Drive in Miami. She'd accompanied Hugh to a conference in South Beach last year. They'd both found the city incredibly gauche and the newly-passed ordinance allowing nude sunbathing was ridiculous and unsanitary.

Yet, here she was. The resolution was incredible. A teen girl, modestly clad in a thong bikini, retrieved a volleyball from the footpath and raced back to her game. Sunlight glinted off the rhinestones of a passing woman's purse and cast rainbows on the ceiling of the room. Arabella reached to remove her glasses – her usual method of consuming virtual reality – before remembering she wasn't wearing any.

Turning her back on the glare of the window, she was confronted by a Fauvist interpretation of the muted impressionist color palette she'd used to decorate Hugh's office. One wall was acid yellow, the others, bright orange.

The living room was even worse. The elegant Louis XIV furniture she'd spent a fortune to ship from London was now a collection of blocky, modernist eyesores. A simple, square light fixture replaced the beautiful cut crystal chandelier she'd won at auction. Had Hugh lost his mind?

Eyes aching from this onslaught, she returned to the bathroom to again splash her face, but, where was it? Not the bathroom – thankfully Hugh hadn't changed anything there – but her face? This was a real mirror, not a screen, and she stared straight through herself to the spectrum of beige towels on the wall behind her. She held up her hands – nothing.

Oh god, she'd gotten a bad pair of lenses. This was why the EU hadn't approved them yet. Was it too late to get them removed? The nanobots needed 24 hours to bond with her eye tissue.

Back in the office, she tried to find the troubleshooting guide on the charging station but the menus cascaded into infinity. She needed help.

Mrs. Constantino answered the door so quickly she must have been standing beside it.

"I'm so sorry," Arabella began, but Mrs. Constantino needed no explanation.

"Come in, dear."

She ushered Arabella into a large, clean living room. Framed photographs of buildings covered the six-meter high walls.

Arabella gaped. "I didn't know any of the apartments had such high ceilings."

Mrs. Constantino smiled. "My husband was a builder. *The* builder, in this case. He gave us the best unit. Would you like a tour?"

Arabella contemplated her invisible feet. "Maybe later. Right now I need help resetting my lenses. Something is wrong."

Mrs. Constantino crooked a finger. "Come to my room. We'll fix you up."

Her bedroom was as neat and tasteful as the living room. Arabella couldn't reconcile this walking pile of rags with the upscale furniture that surrounded her, and the cats she was sure infested the place had yet to make an appearance.

Mrs. Constantino gestured to a rig similar to Hugh's. "Lean in and I'll talk you through it."

A few minutes later, Arabella hurried to a large white and gold mirror and looked with relief into her own red-veined eyes. "Thank you so much. I downloaded my husband's settings and..."

Mrs. Constantino shushed her and took her arm. "Let's have a drink."

"Oh no, I–"

"I insist."

Arabella, surprised by the strength of the woman's grip, allowed herself to be led back to the living room. Mrs. Constantino mixed and poured two martinis with the ease of a hotel bartender.

"What was wrong with your lenses?" she asked, once she and Arabella were seated.

Arabella sipped tentatively. She usually drank white wine. "Well, the apartment was different, but that wasn't the real problem. I couldn't see myself!" She held out a slim, manicured hand. Still there.

Mrs. Constantino laughed, a disturbing half-cough, half-chortle. "Oh honey. Finish that drink and come here."

She swallowed hers in a gulp and waited for Arabella to choke down a bit more of the astringent liquid.

Back in the bedroom, Mrs. Constantino pointed to the charging station. "Get back on there. Choose 'Charles' from the settings menu. Don't worry, we'll put you back to basics after that."

Arabella did, hesitantly. Once her lenses were updated, she stepped back and faced a beautiful, lithe, 20 year-old woman with waist-length black hair.

The woman gazed at her with bewitching, long-lashed brown eyes. Smiling coquettishly, she turned slowly, showing off the kind of figure Arabella failed to attain despite hours a day at the gym.

"Your lenses aren't broken, honey," the beautiful woman proclaimed in an incongruously weary, feathery voice. "Your husband hasn't decided what you look like yet."

Arabella recalled the Miami beach scene, the garish colors in Hugh's office, the altered furniture in the living room, and her own invisibility.

"Unfortunately," she replied, "I'm afraid he has."

M. Luke McDonell is a San Francisco-based writer and designer. Her near-future fiction explores the effects of technology on individuals and society, with particular focus on the growing power of corporations and the associated voluntary and involuntary loss of rights and privacy.

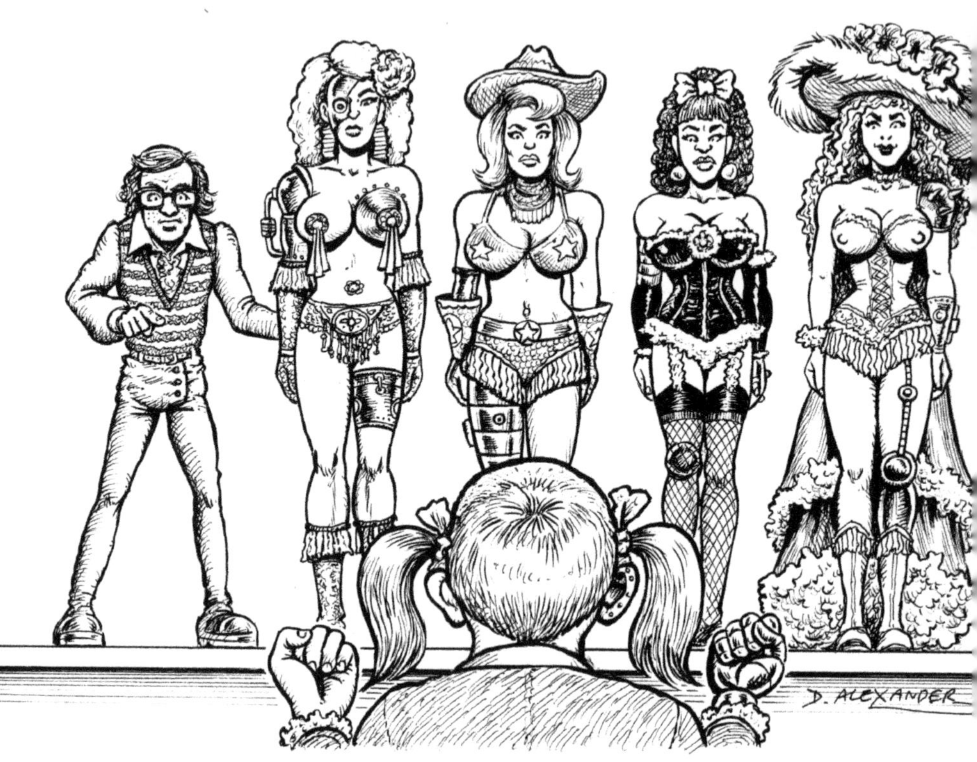

The Brat and the Burly Qs

The Brat and the Burly Qs

David Perlmutter

1.

It seemed like the usual scenario: fly in, tell the bad guy he sucks, stomp him up a bit, and "save the day", as they put it. But there's always a sort of complication involved before you can go ahead and restore order, and this was a bit more unusual than most.

First, allow me to introduce myself, as it's likely we've never met or spoken before this time, right?

My given name, such as it is, is Precious XY-300. The reason being is that I come from a planet (*yes,* I'm an *alien*) where the natives have half their bodies made out of metal on account of our evolution to the climate – you don't see it on me so much 'cause I painted my mechanical parts so that they'd look more "human". I'm here on your Earth, and going under the cover name Precious O'Reilly, on account of some skullduggery in my homeland I'd rather not go into now. Too painful. The point is, I ended up in your solar system, and I now fight crime etc. within it as the Brat. That accounts for the "B" on my shirt, in case you were wondering.

Now, you might *also* be wondering what a "three year old girl", blonde haired, blue eyed, wearing a blue wool jacket, white skirt and boots, and the aforementioned shirt, is doing here in a bar unaccompanied, and drinking a beer. Well, let's get something straight, pal. I'm *not* a three year old girl! I can pass as one, as you'll soon see, but, in all other respects, I am an *adult.* Everyone on my planet is the same, diminutive size as me through youth and adulthood. Anyone over 4 feet tall is considered as much of a freak of nature as someone who weighed 400 pounds or more would be amongst you guys. Still, people see me as a little girl and treat me like it. Until I open my mouth or throw a punch at them, that is.

Sorry for the info dump, but it's necessary to understand the story I'm gonna tell ya. I don't want the good readers of "Super Heroics Illustrated" getting the wrong idea about me, after all. And it's a sign of good faith on your part that you can keep that thing going, considering how many of us don't want to talk to you. But my friends say you're legit, so I guess I can trust you. Up to a point!

Anyhow, this is what happened on Mars:

2.

I was alerted to the situation by my associates in the Interplanetary League Of Girls With Guns (referring to our collective Herculean musculature, but, in my case, also to my built-in weaponry). The five of us, as soon as we knew of each other's existence, struck up a gentlelady's agreement that we'd each patrol a particular sector of the universe, and wouldn't interfere with each other's business unless things got too hot for us to handle alone. (Like it does, once in a while.) Anyway, they told me that that son of a bitch Machine Gun Steinberg had managed to escape from his confinement on Earth, overpowered the nearest set of security guards, and re-established his burlesque business in the ugly imitation French Quarter they set up in New New Orleans, so named as it's at the extreme southern tip of the newly terraformed Earth colony in the shadow of Olympus Mons.

This rattled my coils. Who do you think was responsible for putting that guy in jail in the first place? Me, that's who! And thus, by the informal ILGWG rules, I had to put him *back* there. Not that I *minded* that!

Steinberg, as you probably know, was the man who single-handedly revolutionized the "art" of "burlesque" (i.e. stupid young humans taking their clothes off) by managing to create pliable mechanical strippers for the first time. Or, I should say, *part* mechanical. He scurried around human graveyards, finding undecomposed human body parts, and then had them welded together with a variety of mechanical features to make them....interesting enough for the "patrons" of the "art". Electronic legs, remote controlled boobs, and so on. Naturally, the girls have automatic brains, so that they only do as they're told all the time. No free-thinking real human woman I know would actually get involved with that crap unless they were really desperate for cash.

However, he made money. And aroused the ire of feminists, besides. And, ultimately, I had to step in and destroy his assets before anything apocalyptic happened. 'Cause he was actually getting women coming to him for jobs, women who wanted a mechanical transplant added to their natural bodies. They were lining up outside his club for work on their own free will. Jeez!

Thus, I found myself flying to Mars. (Yeah, *that* type of flying, of course. I'm a superhero, after all.) That John Gray fellow was damn right when he said men came from Mars. Imagine Texas, or better yet, your average big city downtown on a Saturday night, and that's exactly what Mars has become ever since the creation of synthetic water allowed that liquid to flow through those mythical canals and make Ray Bradbury's dreams a reality. Naturally, you have settlements that resemble the Wild West in the days when it actually *was* wild. Like New New Orleans. Ugly as hell, and not the place that even a three year old girl can walk around for fear of having her feminine virtue permanently immolated.

Not that I'm one of *those*.

3.

I made New New Orleans in good time, and was soon in the ugly imitation French Quarter, with Martian natives coerced into adopting phony Creole and Cajun *patois* and strutting around like they owned the place. (Two words: *em-barrasing!*). I was soon able to find Steinberg's, owing to the giant neon sign displaying both his name and the backside of a giant woman with outlined 3D boobs.

As Fat Albert and the Cosby Kids would say- *no class*!

I walked to the front door and started to put on my best three year old girl act, with voice and gestures to match, in hopes the bouncer would let me in.

"Is my *mommy* in there?" I piped up.

The guy apparently couldn't *see* me, on account of the fact that he actually started walking around and asking "Who said that?" I wasn't surprised.With his gut being so big, he probably hadn't seen his own feet for some time.

In any event, I repeated my question, in a shriller and more pleadingly desperate tone. That time, he knew I was there and looked at me.

"You *want* somethin', lil' girl?" he asked me, contemptuously.

"I wan' my *mommy*!" I said, tears coming to my cheeks.

"She ain't here!"

"Mommy said wait out here while she takes her clothes off to earn money for her meth…."

"Ain't none of my concern, kid."

"An'…..An'……I'm so all alone…..an' scared….'cause Daddy gonna beat her up if he found she spen' th' rent money on *meth* again…."

"You hard of hearin', *brat*? I *said* she ain't *here*!"

Well, that *did* it! I'm a brat, all right, but only with a capital B, not a small one. I shucked my coat off, hardened my expression, grabbed his ankle with my super-powered mechanical right arm, and made a fist with my organic left one.

"Listen, buddy!" I exclaimed in my natural voice. "You might think I'm *a* brat, but I'm *The* Brat! You *understand?* I'm the most powerful three year old in the universe, and I can knock you *six ways from Sunday* if I take a *dIs*-like to you. Now, your *employer* is a wanted fugitive from Earth, and I intend to take him back where he belongs. You *dig* that, MOTHERFUCKER?"

Having said my peace, I threw the dude over my shoulder, and he ran away from me like the beaten dog he was. There now remained only Steinberg, and I proceeded to enter his establishment to silence him.

4.

I brushed through the informal anterooms and entered the main ballroom chamber of Steinberg's joint. It was typical Wild West bedlam: half-mechanical girls parading around in next to nothing on the stage, or sat on the exclusively male patrons' tables, chairs and laps. They, of course, were doing everything possible to encourage the drinking, dancing and stripping done by the girls. I, however, would not.

"*STEINBERG*!" I screamed, with fists clenched.

Everything went dead silent, and everyone looked at me, like in Western movies when the bad guy walks into the saloon looking for the hero. That's the way it was, only in this case, the hero came looking for the villain.

I walked over to a table of miscreants, who were drunk, like they usually are.

"Get out," I drawled humorlessly.

"Come *on*, man!" one of them said. "We just wanna…"

I gave them no chance to explain. I pressed a few invisible buttons on my mechanical arm. The hand temporarily raised, and a jet of flame burst out and destroyed the chairs they had been sitting on. (They moved to escape it, of course.) Then my hand snapped back into place.

"I *SAID* 'GET OUT'!"

The men – all of them – got out of the building, leaving only the puzzled looking girls. Then Steinberg entered, having been in the back.

"Jesus Christ," he shouted. "How many times have I gotta tell ya…."

His blood turned cold and his words stopped as soon as he saw me.

"What the hell are *you* doing here?" he said. "I didn't think you supes had any authority off of Earth…"

"You poor, dumb, delusional *putz*!" I shot back. "Don't you realize I can be anywhere I want, any *time* I want? And that means I can collar your deluded *ass* any time I want, too! You disappoint me, Steinberg. My fellow heroes have much more imposing, threatening, *masculine* foes to deal with, but *I* have to settle for a third rate Woody Allen impersonator!"

He cursed me violently, up and down, in Yiddish, thinking I didn't know the language, and, thus, would not know my honor had been insulted. But I *did* know the language, and fluently at that. This I demonstrated not only repudiating what he had just said about me, but by further compromising his own limited integrity.

"Bah!" he said, switching back to English. "It's time I was rid of you. Burly Qs!"

At this moment, all of Steinberg's cyborg automatons came to attention, and stood stiff as soldiers in a line in front of me.

"Steinberg," I asked rhetorically, "are you *kidding* me? You know perfectly well that I…."

"….am stronger and more powerful than any other *goyim* child of your age in the universe, on account of your alien birth and mechanical 'enhancements'." He interrupted me, reproducing my usual intro spiel to opponents (but adding the *goyim* to spite me.) "*Oy*! Do I *ever* know that! But that's why I had the Avicenna Development Corporation fix this lot up for me – so I could *defend* myself from you!"

"Avicenna?" I spat on the ground to indicate my contempt for them. "Those *hacks*? They couldn't build a decent robot without *killing* people to do it!"

"You won't think so once the girls get through with you."

"I doubt that they have much on them. Just like *you*."

"*Fine,* girlfriend! You *asked* for it. Burly Qs- *attack!*"

The girls shed their humanized exteriors to reveal guns, weapons and ammo encased in their hair, eyes, teeth, noses, hands, arms, legs, feet and even their you-know-whats. And, at their master's command, they proceeded to attack me *en masse.*

I responded by employing my own weapons to fire at them, though I did so more strategically, dropping, rolling and tucking (like my opponents probably did onstage) to avoid their weapons, and then staggering them with shots from my arm-gun when I saw a chance. That allowed me to pick a few of them off, and they exploded, inert, into mounds of useless flesh and metal within seconds.

The three remaining half-mechanical bitches ganged up on me from behind. One encased me in a powerful bear hug I couldn't break, another bounced out a mechanical net, which the first one threw me into and tied up above me, and then the third one, while I was trying to open the net at the top, did a Spider-Man with her wrist and shot some piping hot, bubbling grey liquid at my mechanical side. I wasn't able to move in time, so it covered me all over. Holy shit, did it *sting*!

"JESUS *CHRIST*!" I ejaculated, in the midst of my pain.

Now, as I am normally invulnerable to the works of Man, this came as quite a shock to me. I soon reasoned what was going on as I saw my powerful mechanical arm give off sparks, shut down, and go limp, and my bionic right leg go likewise. Steinberg had, likely through his connections, managed to find a store of liquid mercury – the one material in the universe to which natives of my planet are vulnerable – and surreptitiously charged one of his robot-strippers with it to wound me. That he did, and soon as he did, the three of them took advantage of my reduced circumstances and started beating the shit out of me.

While I took their hits, I lamented my fate and beat myself up mentally.

What the hell am I gonna DO? I said to myself. My guns and weapons are gone. I've just got my body and my wits, and that might not be enough.

Yet that stereotypical minute of self-doubt existed for only a couple of seconds. I suddenly remembered what I *did* have. A *brain.* The mightiest weapon of them all. A brain will get you out of things even superpowers can't, if you use it and nurture it right like I do. Sure, I know that those cyborg types have brains, too, but they're *fake* brains, run on electrical impulses rather than natural nerve generators. No substitute.

This I showed them with the still active – and still powerful – left, organic side of my body. Once I had freed myself from their trap, I dislocated their mechanical parts from their organic ones. That being done, I caught Steinberg trying to make his exit out the back door.

"No, you fucking WON'T!" I snapped.

I overtook him, lifted him above my head, and threw him into one of the abandoned tables of the club. He was down and out.

I proceeded to give him the same ruminations on the brain I just gave you, as well as more profanity laced ones about how *important* the metal half of my body *is* to me, how he was going to personally pay cash money to replace every single part of me the mercury damaged, and how I was going to personally escort him back to Earth, and jail-after that. I particularly emphasized that he should STAY there if he did not want any more trouble.

"You got any PROBLEMS with that?" I concluded.

He didn't.

5.

Oops. My pager. I gotta go, man. Let me know when the story comes out. And, for *your* sake, it better be *flattering*!

David Perlmutter is a freelance writer based in Winnipeg, Manitoba, Canada. The holder of an MA degree from the Universities of Manitoba and Winnipeg, and a lifelong animation fan, he has published short fiction in a variety of genres for various magazines and anthologies, as well as essays on his favorite topics for similar publishers. He is the author of *America Toons In: A History of Television Animation* (McFarland and Co.), *The Singular Adventures Of Jefferson Ball* (Chupa Cabra House) and *The Pups*

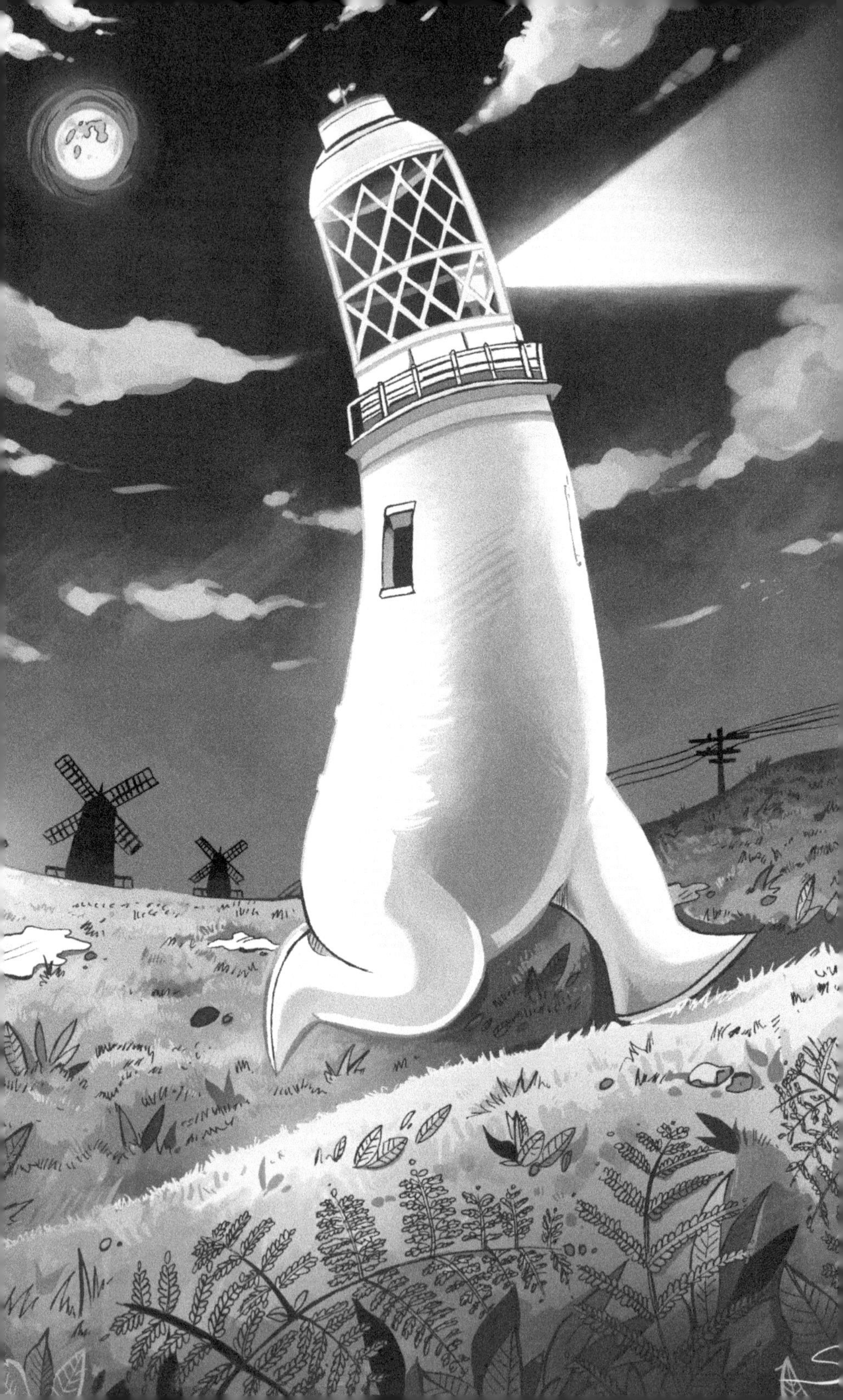

Approaching 43,000 Candles

Guy T Martland

When the moon stopped time, he struck out across a dark blanket of sea. After clambering up the rocky coast, he leapt over the headlands and the fields, past the assembly of ruined tin mines, before moving up the country with long, loping steps. He passed by sleeping villages and stilled towns caught in the stuttering gasps of yesterday evening's revelry. A beam of light shone from his face, illuminating his path, casting the landscape into sharp relief. Sometimes, the moon would help, poking her way between the low clouds that scudded across the nightscape, and he'd dim the projection, letting the heavenly body instead play over the rolling earth that was England.

"The first day of the year," he mused, thinking about the past fifty-two weeks and of any stories he could relay to the others. Not that he had much to tell. He wasn't one of the celebrities like the Bishop Rock, with its rolling slot as a BBC ident. Or La Jument, made popular by that photographer Guichard – she'd been on walls across the land, her keeper poking his head out of the door when the huge wave struck; everyone knew that picture. He remembered the fuss when Virginia Woolf wrote about Godrevy all those years ago. He wasn't like them. At most he'd accumulate modest recognition in a few people's photo albums. The run of popular postcards from the late nineties had even run its course.

He was Round Island, based on the Scillies, like the Bishop. In Cornish, this was 'Golowji an Voth', which was why everyone tended to call him Voth. He was now fully automated—his keeper had left years back, and being in such an inaccessible place, he rarely had visitors, apart from the sea birds. He didn't mind the gulls, but when the puffins came to visit, they kept him awake all day with their incessant chatter.

He walked across Dartmoor, feet crunching through the bracken. He nodded as he passed the telegraph poles and the windmills, although they hadn't been granted access tonight; they were as still as the sheep in the field he tiptoed through. For a moment he thought he saw a light behind him, but it was just the moon reflecting in his glass, as if watching him. He'd thought for a moment it was the Bishop, and began to wonder about when he had left. Once they'd travelled up to the North European conference together, but never again. The house was so full of itself. Voth had moved to the Scillies for a quiet life. They hadn't got on.

Soon he saw other beams flaring across the hills like distant fires. All were converging on the centre of Birmingham for the annual get together. It was always a landlocked destination so no-one became distracted by the sea. Last year it had been Cambridge. He was looking forward to catching up with his old Scottish friends – inveterate drinkers, they'd be the first propping up the bar.

After registering, he took a cursory glance at the series of programmed events. The usual guff about increased mechanisation. There was even a session on the newer radio lighthouses – if you had the money that was the way to go it seemed. Innovations in GPS and the diminishing usefulness of lighthouses were also scheduled. He slid a programme into one of his windows and consulted the course organiser about the evening reception.

As he walked through the city centre, he trod carefully around the huts of the German Christmas market to Temple Row, where the temporary bar had been erected. Skerryvore was already in his cups, shouting loudly at Voth as he entered the open space. A whisky was shortly pressed into his hand and Skerryvore launched into a long anecdote, much of which was hidden behind his thick accent. Despite this, he managed to keep up.

"... these army folk. Lived in my belly while they tried to find the downed Tornado. I thought I could drink, but they put it away."

"Still getting the Stevenson visitors?" asked Voth, as Skerryvore finished his story, slammed his glass on the bar and demanded another.

"Aye. Those literary types show up every once in a while. Keeps things ticking over..."

At that moment, the Bishop sashayed into the bar, La Jument on his arm. He passed his beam over the assembled in an almost condescending manner.

"Wanker," muttered Skerryvore.

"I'm glad it isn't just me who thinks that," said Voth.

"I don't know how you can put up with him all year round..."

"He keeps his distance."

He lost Skerryvore sometime after the reception. The Scot had staggered up to him, suggested they go clubbing, flickering out a strobe of light in anticipation. But after the long trip up, Voth just wanted to head back to the hotel. He left Skerryvore to it, wandering off through unfamiliar strange city streets. After a wrong turning, he found himself somewhere near Gas Street Basin, his light dancing over the Victorian canals.

As he tried to orientate himself, he heard some voices. Peeking around the side of a red brick brewery building, recently converted to expensive flats, he saw three of them in conversation. One was the Bishop, the other two Wolf Rock and Longships, more of the Cornish contingent. The Bishop towered above both of them, his helipad like a mortar board. The other two had a similar, squatter structure, and appeared to be cocking their heads up to their taller colleague.

"In the July fog, we'll do it," said Bishop, his well-bred tones reverberating around the space.

"The tankers will be passing closest on the 7th, 12th and 18th," said either Longships or Wolf Rock.

"Co-ordinated switch off," said either Wolf Rock or Longships.

"The tide will take it straight over to the rocks near Tater Du. She'll be blamed."

Voth felt condensation creeping over his lens. They were planning an act of sabotage? But why? What had the lovely Tater Du done to them? Voth racked his brains, but couldn't remember anything about the relative newcomer to the Cornish coast. He tried to still his breathing, his mirrors spinning faster in the dark.

They seemed to turn away after that, their voices lost behind the winter wind that had crept up, whistling up from the Black Country, thrumming around his ears. When he next poked his glass around the corner, they had gone. He wandered over to where they had been standing, hoping to catch a memory of their words on the wind, but the pattern of sound had dissipated.

He slept fitfully, waking when he remembered their plan fitted in perfectly with his planned Summer service, when he'd be out of action over the fortnight they'd mentioned. After a light breakfast, he wound his way back to the conference centre, trying to keep his shutters open as he attended the seminar on radio technologies. The morning wound into lunch, where he once again found Skerryvore propping up the bar, already on his second pint of the day.

"It's only Deuchars, IPA. A session ale," he muttered to Round Island's admonishment. "And anyways, we're on holiday!"

"Listen, Skerryvore. I was wondering if you knew anything about Tater Du …"

"The Cornish strumpet, you mean?"

"I suppose so …"

"Well, after she and Wolf broke it off–"

"She was with Wolf?" interrupted Voth.

"Aye. Back in the early eighties."

"But she … she's a lot younger than him."

"He was cut up about it, I think. She left him for Mevagissey."

"Hmm …"

"What's the problem? You fancy her?"

"No … it's just …," he started, before outlining the conversation he'd heard the night before.

"And you can't change the service dates?"

"I could try, but …"

"I don't trust him, that Bishop. You remember when that French lighthouse was found, ten years ago, after the conference in Paris …"

Voth remembered this all too well. He reminded Skerryvore that he'd been the first to find the string of stones, the shattered lens. And the bulb which had apparently burnt its life out. There'd been an inquest, the verdict: suicide. Although, some suspicions had been raised, dragging out proceedings. Being the first on the scene, fingers had pointed at Voth. The rumour mill was set in motion, information misdirected, as if someone wanted to divert any blame – and it seemed that the lighthouse responsible for these rumours was the Bishop.

When they'd returned to real time, it was reported that an unusually strong wave had pulled the stricken French lighthouse into the depths of the ocean. But that hadn't been the end of it - the moon had expressed her annoyance at the length of the hearing by curtailing the annual conference for the two following years. Voth returned to Round Island, his reputation tarnished, guilty purely by his association with events.

"You really thinking they are planning on sabotage?" asked Skerryvore, the next day. He'd just enjoyed a quick whisky chaser before reverting to the Deuchars.

"I don't know. Maybe I misheard it? It was windy…"

"Sounds like they were up to something… Whatever it was, it was no good."

"Another one?"

"And why not?"

With hangovers, they departed the conference the following morning, Skerryvore joining Stroma and the rest of the Stevenson flock for the trip back up north. As Voth plodded across the countryside towards Cornwall, he wondered about why the Bishop would choose to help out the Wolf in this way. He swung down to the south coast, passing where Tater Du had re-established herself, plunging her feet back into the comfort of the Earth.

A ruptured tanker would destroy the coastline. He imagined the thick, black slick swallowing all the sea-birds, engulfing the tourist beaches with oily gunk. And all for an act of petty revenge against a former lover? There had to be more to it that that… He scanned the horizon, searching for an answer. In response, the moon appeared, reflected in the sea below, her scowl reminding him that he had to get home. An hour or so later, he had returned to Round Island. The moon winked out and time began once again. His light powered on and began its cycle, scanning the horizon like a searchlight for clues to the mystery.

The months passed, Winter's weathering storms moving quickly into spring. The puffins returned about the same time the rock moss began to flower, little blooms popping up all over Round Island, lending it a purple shade. And then suddenly it was July and as predicted, mist fell, enshrouding the islands with its pall. Foghorns bleated plaintively at each other through the blind light.

And just as he was getting into his stride, the scheduled maintenance happened. Voth was stripped bare, his bulb removed, his shutters and mirrors unclipped and examined. One day he heard the men who were fiddling with his insides talking.

"Funding cuts, isn't it …"

"What's that?"

"The Bishop. They say he'll fall into the sea if they don't do that maintenance."

"It'll cost a fair few bob…"

"You can say that again. Best do it now, while the weather's good."

"They'll wait until it turns, mark my words…"

And then he thought he saw it. The Bishop and his friends were to fail on purpose. The coastline would be damaged, but Tater Du would soak up most of the blame – it would mostly fall on her patch. Their status would be elevated, they would be regarded as essential. The maintenance would happen sooner. That was assuming they somehow managed to sabotage the GPS systems as well. Did they also want to attract the usual Cornish tourists? Pull them to unspoiled Scilly instead so they could bask in human admiration? Was that another part of their plan? There had to be another way, he thought. Why all this senseless damage to the coast?

The 7th of July rolled around, and the 12th—both nights were clear; the stars bright and almost three dimensional, scattered over the sky like a sprinkling of fine powder. But as the 18th approached, Voth couldn't see more that a few metres through the thick fog. Even his platform wasn't visible. The nearby Agnes was useless as well, her light guttering after a few hundred meters. The Bishop, whose glare usually sliced through the fog like a meteor across the heavens, didn't seem to be working. When he tested the GPS and found it was down, a sense of something like fear collected along his spiral staircase.

"*Skerryvore, it's happening. Thick fog. GPS has somehow been disrupted. Their plans are reaching fruition,*" he emailed up to his Hebridean friend.

"*Hang in there Voth,*" was the short reply.

He listened, his hearing more acute in the fog. In the distance, he could hear the wail of foghorns.

And then, as if from nowhere, beads of brilliant ethereal light appeared in the mist. The tanker, which was about to smash against the rocks, changed course, following the makeshift beacons. A second tanker, also about to prang the North Cornish coast, later described the sight: "*Like chunks of the full moon had been sent down, to guide us on our way.*"

Months later, the plot was unravelled. The Stevenson collective had decided to inform the moon and the moon was angry: angry with The Bishop Rock. It took her a great effort to deal with human affairs, especially to deal with errant lighthouses wilfully switching themselves off and disrupting GPS systems for their own egregious purposes. Nefarious. All three of them, complicit in this crime, were barred from attending the conference for the next twenty years.

The near misses were logged and described by the two captains. The 'power cut' which had affected the Cornish trio, combined with the temporary failure of the GPS, meant that humans began to take the remaining lighthouses more seriously. The Bishop, The Wolf and the Longships got their wishes for upgrades. And Tater Du had escaped unscathed, to Wolf's chagrin, Voth presumed. Added to which, the surge of interest in lighthouses had resulted in the BBC commissioning a drama series set on Round Island itself.

At the next conference, Voth was lauded as a hero. He found himself enjoying his new status, although mindful of The Bishop, retained his modest nature. And it turned out Skerryvore had been wrong about Tater Du – her liaison with Mevagissey had been brief and unfulfilling. She looked at him with new eyes. They swapped numbers. He returned to Round Island a changed lighthouse.

As he sat on the hump of rock, casting his beam over the fishermen and trawlers of the Scillies, and even further into the major shipping lanes, he felt a strong sense of pride. The moon appeared from behind a cloud and winked at him. He looked out across the islands and realised that this was happiness. His future was bright: brighter than his current 42,945 candles, he mused to himself.

Guy T Martland is a British SF writer and poet based in Bournemouth. He has published short stories in a number of magazines, including *Perihelion SF*, *Encounters*, *Albedo 1*, *Fiction Vortex* and *Imaginalis*. His first SF novel '*The Scion*', will be published by *Safkhet* later this year.

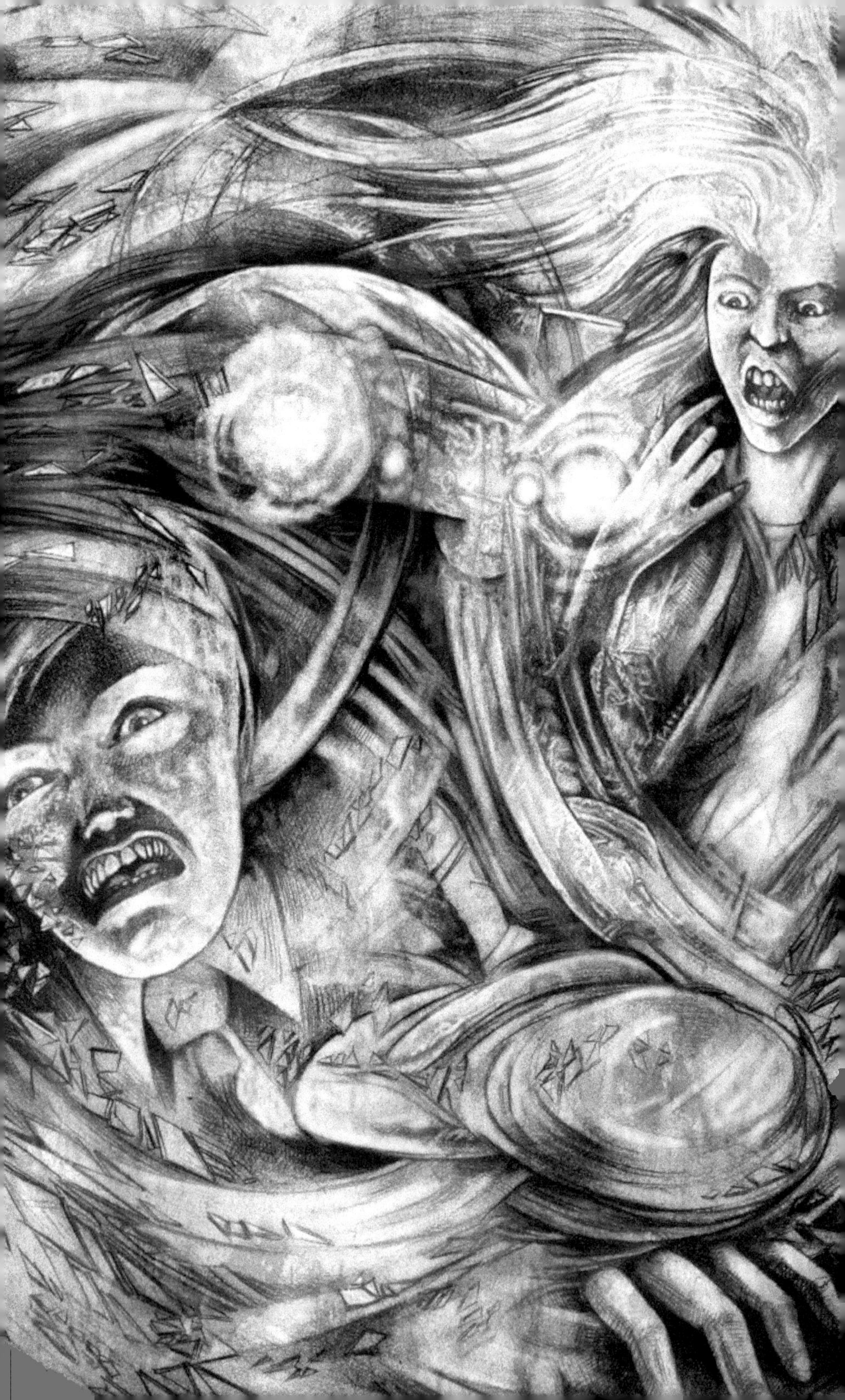

Broken Glass

Joseph L Kellogg

Glasses clinked in five identical sets of hands, between five identical husbands and wives, distinguished by only their clothes and the colored bands they wore around their wrists. RedBrian watched all the other Brians like fragments of a carnival mirror, reflections of himself from other universes, moving out of sync with him as they talked over the noise of the bar, wishing each other a happy birthday. Five Pats echoed congratulations at them, blond hair shimmering in the light from neon beer signs. A hand reached over and pulled his face to the side.

"Happy Birthday," Janice said, kissing him briefly on the lips. The sole brunette at the table, she nuzzled his nose for a moment, then pushed back her chair. "I'm going to make room for another drink."

YellowBrian leaned over and blew beer-soaked breath into RedBrian's ear as he spoke. "So what's the news with Janice?" he asked, chuckling. "You ever gonna make an honest woman out of her?"

"Eventually, I guess," RedBrian said. "I'm just waiting for the right time, you know?"

"You've been dating for what, three years now? What else could you be waiting for?"

At the end of the table GreenPat brushed her hair back, and words popped up unbidden from RedBrian's subconscious. I'm waiting for her. Just behind her ear he caught a glimpse of the scar from that car wreck when Pat was a kid. Each of the different Pats had almost identical scars, hidden under their hair, reminders of their brush with death. All of them except for RedPat; in a different universe, a different song was playing on the radio, she was dancing to a different beat, and the shard of glass hit her in a different spot, cutting right through her jugular instead. RedPat, the girl he was supposed to marry, was currently drifting toward the bottom of the Pacific Ocean, her cremated body fertilizing seaweed instead of wishing him another happy birthday.

YellowBrian interrupted his brooding. "I've heard her talking at the office," he said. "She's getting tired of waiting for you to pop the question. You'd better make your move before she does, if you know what I mean."

"You really think so?" asked RedBrian, dragging his finger listlessly through the icing on his slice of cake. Red mentally kicked himself for not being ready to get married. Janice was a great girl, and in other circumstances he probably could have lived quite happily. But when the other universes were discovered, and Slide Stations started popping up around the world, he met his five doppelgängers and saw how nauseatingly happy they were with their Pats. After a few months of searching for his own, all he'd found was the small plaque in the cemetery and a couple of parents who still cried over their little lost angel.

Janice sidled back up to Red at the table, and brushed a lock of hair from his forehead. "Are you feeling alright?" she asked.

"I think I might be coming down with something, actually," he replied. "Sorry. You mind if I go ahead and take you back to the Station?"

"No, of course not," Janice said coolly, scratching at her yellow wristband.

"We might as well catch a ride with you," said YellowBrian as he slammed down the last of his beer and helped YellowPat to her feet. "I've got to be at work bright and early tomorrow. Come on, sweetie."

As soon as RedBrian climbed into the driver's seat, his car smelled the alcohol on his breath and switched to automatic control.

"Would You Like To Go Home?" the computer asked in the staccato tones of piecemeal voice recordings.

"No," Red muttered. "Take us to the Slide Station first."

The car rumbled to life and began maneuvering out of the parking garage, while Red leaned his seat back until he hit YellowBrian's knees behind him. After a few minutes, they'd escaped downtown and were cruising down the highway toward the next city over. Janice turned around in her seat up front and wrinkled her forehead at YellowBrian.

"Are you still working on that client you went to lunch with the other day? The Brazilian company, right?"

"Yeah, I've just gotta work out-"

Headlights. Spinning. Flying. Glass rained on the left side of Red's face, and Janice's hair swung in a circle as the car rolled once and thudded back down onto the wheels. Something hissed in the hood, and hot blood coated Red's left arm. He groaned and turned his head. Janice and YellowPat were only scratched up, but unconscious from the impact. He kicked open his door, crushed by the collision with the other car, and stumbled to the backseat to check on YellowBrian. His stomach twisted when he looked in the broken-out window. A fist-sized shard of glass protruded from Yellow's throat, and more blood flowed over his pale, motionless body.

Red stood dumbfounded for a moment. He remembered that the car's computer would have already called for an ambulance. There were only a few minutes before emergency services would arrive, but YellowBrian was already long gone. Still slightly dazed from shock, blood loss, and alcohol, he pried open the back door, dragged Yellow out, and started taking off both of their clothes and armbands.

Brian woke up, his arms and legs aching, with the dull glow of fluorescent lights above him in an antiseptic white ceiling. Someone off to his side squeezed his hand.

"Sweetie?" Pat's face leaned down over his and gave him a weak smile. "How are you feeling?"

Brian's eyes darted down to Pat's wristband. Yellow.

"I hurt like hell," Brian said. "What happened?"

"There was an accident on the highway," Pat said. "Do you remember anything?"

"I... I think I remember getting hit, spinning. Was I driving?"

"No, sweetie, Red was driving, but it wasn't his fault. He was on automatic, and another car jumped the median."

Brian glanced down at his own wrist, pulling his hand out from under the hospital blanket. Yellow. But he was RedBrian, wasn't he? "Was anyone else hurt?"

"Janice and I are fine," Pat answered. "But Red... They found him in the front seat; he was dead when the paramedics got there."

Brian remembered vague images of looking at one of his doubles in the back seat, covered with blood. He glanced down at his wrist again. If he was Yellow, why did he remember being Red? The haze started to lift in his mind, and he remembered the feeling of wrapping a blood-soaked shirt around himself on the highway, the warmth of the fluid shielding him from the chill of the night. He remembered pulling off his wristband... oh, God.

Pat brushed aside his hair, and he smiled. It felt so natural, like this was how it was meant to be. While he'd been drunk, he must have done something he never would have done sober, but he was thankful for it. All these years, he'd had to watch all of his doubles with their Pats. Now here she was doting on him.

Outside his vision, the door latch clicked, and Pat turned to look. "Janice, he's awake," she said.

Janice walked into the room and onto Brian's left side. Her face was covered with scratches, some of them bandaged. They didn't seem to detract from her prettiness nearly as much as her red, swollen eyes. She crossed her arms tightly across her chest, sniffed back some tears, and squeaked out a cursory "Hi, Brian."

"Hi, Janice." Brian scratched carefully around the stitches on his arm. "Look... I'm sorry."

"It wasn't your fault."

Brian didn't answer.

A few days later, the rubber tip of Brian's crutch dug into the false grass under the collapsible pavilion as he plodded down the center aisle toward the coffin. He wasn't sure where to sit, but then he spotted the rest of his doubles lined up in the front row, and he followed their lead. He took a seat next to YellowPat. His Pat. Rain pattered on the tarp above them, and the folding chairs sat slightly off-kilter on the uneven ground beneath the green carpet. Everyone sat in a cocoon of plastic, while nature shuddered and cried around them. Brian set his crutches down next to his chair, and caught Janice's eye across the aisle.

Part of Brian wanted to run up to her, take her into his arms, and tell her that he was still alive, and it was someone else in that coffin. But it was too late for that. A man got up and spoke, a preacher that Brian barely remembered from his days in elementary school. After a few opening remarks and a reading from the Psalms, he stepped aside to let Brian's brother Pete give the eulogy. Brian chuckled at each story of their childhood exploits, but his heart seized at each one, wondering if YellowBrian had the same stories. Did he even have a brother? He wasn't sure.

Pat reached over and took Brian's hand. He twitched, almost pulling back on reflex.But no, she meant to take his hand – he was her husband. He closed his eyes and repeated that fact to himself silently, over and over. I am YellowBrian. I am YellowBrian. I am YellowBrian. He rubbed his hands together to ward off the cold of the rain around them, and was reminded of the plain gold wedding band he wore now. 'Til death do us part.'

As YellowBrian's—his—brother stepped away from the microphone, the mourners lined up to pay their last respects. Brian looked down into the casket as he passed, looked at his own face lying silently on velvet, and he wasn't sure who was dead and who was alive. Soon the undertaker lowered the body into the grave, and began piling dirt on top of it. Each thud of wet earth resonated in Brian's chest like a shotgun blast, and he wanted to run to the grave, crying that he'd dropped his keys inside, anything that would make them stop. As long as he was above ground, Brian could tell everyone what had happened, swap the wristbands back, and crawl into the casket where he belonged. But Pat tugged at his hand

and led him away to the car. She drove them to the luncheon, where they served three different kinds of casserole.

A week later, Brian stared at the invoices on his computer screen. He wished he could ask one of his doubles what to do. Even though he had the same job as all the others, their account numbers and names were different. But he couldn't concentrate on it anyway. All he could think about was the barely audible sound of muffled tears from Janice's desk two cubicles down. He remembered wishing before that they lived in the same universe, and he didn't have to pay for a Slide every time he wanted to see her. Now she was working just a few feet away, and he didn't know what to say, or if he wanted to say anything.

After a few more hours of staring blankly at paperwork he didn't recognize, Brian counted the seconds on the clock until it reached closing time, then shut down his computer, grabbed his jacket, walked down the hall and into the parking garage. As he trudged through the dimly-lit concrete path, he passed Janice's car, where she leaned listlessly against the door, her forehead pressed against the window with lethargic apathy.

"How are you doing?" Brian asked. It was the first thing he'd said to her all day.

"Bad," she said with a harsh sniffle. "I just don't know where to go from here."

"What do you mean?"

"I thought we were meant for each other. His was the only Pat that died in that car wreck as a girl, but I was the only Janice that survived mine. It had symmetry, you know?"

"And now... he died in a car wreck," Brian said flatly.

"I guess that's symmetrical too," Janice growled.

"Is there anything I can do?" Brian stepped forward and leaned against the car next to her.

"I think I just need space. I can't look at your face without thinking it's him, even just for a second, and... and I don't think I can handle that."

"If it makes you feel better, I think he wanted to propose." It was true. He thought that he had wanted to propose. "He just didn't know how to do it."

"It doesn't count for much now, does it?"

"No, I suppose not."

They stood silently and the roar of car engines echoing in the parking garage died down as everyone else started their commute. Brian gave her a pained smile, then began to slink away when she grabbed his arm.

"Wait." She looked up anxiously into his face. "I never really got to say goodbye. Can I...?" She stood up on her toes and kissed Brian briefly, her lips tinged with the salt of tears and sweetness of chapstick. "I'm sorry, I probably shouldn't have-"

Brian clutched the back of her head and pulled her into him. He kissed her, sucking at her lips like they were his last chance of survival. At first she resisted, but her hands soon wrapped around his back and she sighed with painful relief. With blindly groping hands, she opened the back door of her car, and they fell into the seat. Something in the back of Brian's mind pointed out that where she had been his consolation prize before, now he was hers. But that thought was pushed away as her clothes slipped off, hastily revealing her familiar warmth.

That night, a buckle jangled as Brian dropped his bag to the ground by the front door. A plate of spaghetti sat at the table, the clumps of Parmesan cheese stained orange from the sauce. Pat drifted in from the kitchen, her makeup already wiped off.

"Hey, sweetie," she said weakly, kissing him on the cheek. Her lips burned, and Brian worried that she would taste Janice on him. "I'm sorry I didn't wait for you, but I didn't know when you'd be home."

"I just... needed to take a detour. Clear my head."

"I know." She wrapped her arms around him, and buried her face against his neck. "I know this has been hard on you. I wish there was something I could do to make you feel better."

Brian lifted his hand, looking at the reflection of the light on his wedding ring. She was his wife now, and this was the most they had touched since the hospital. Everything he had ever wanted was in his arms right now, but he couldn't stop thinking about Janice.

"I just need time," he said, pulling away from Pat's embrace. "I'm going to the study to think, maybe watch TV. I'll join you for bed later."

The battered old recliner in the study was unfamiliar, and springs poked him in unexpected places when he sat. He could still feel Janice all over him, their mingled sweat tainting his clothes. Had he cheated on Pat? He wore the ring, but he wasn't the one that made that promise to her. Brian took the ring off and turned it absentmindedly in his fingers. He thought he could see flecks of dried blood still stuck on the inside, but his gut told him those should have worn off already. He wanted to call up one of his doubles and ask his advice, but he knew that wouldn't help. They had no experience here; whatever he did, he was on his own.

Brian grabbed a coat from the closet, reading the label on the inside of the collar before putting it on. Cecil Lawrence. Lawrence was a good name. Maybe he could become a Lawrence. Not Larry. Lawrence.

He crept into the kitchen, scrawled a note, and left it on the table. His —no, not his, YellowBrian's—wedding ring plunked down on top of it. Stepping out into the night, he closed the front door as quietly as he could. The sky was clear and full of moonlight as he drove to the Slide Station, and it was still clear on the Red side. When he reached the cemetery, Brian didn't need his flashlight to find his way to the fresh grave, green shoots just peaking up out of the damp brown soil.

With slow and steady strokes, Brian dug a small hole on top of the grave with his bare hands, dropping the dirt carefully to the side with each handful. Then he placed the yellow wristband inside, and filled it back in. It didn't occur to him until he was back in the car that they wouldn't let him back through the Slide Station without a wristband. But at least he was in his own universe now, and if he never saw one of his doubles again, Lawrence could figure things out.

Joseph L. Kellogg works as an environmental chemist by day, and writes speculative fiction by night. He lives in Northeast Tennessee with his wife and absolutely, positively, no cats.

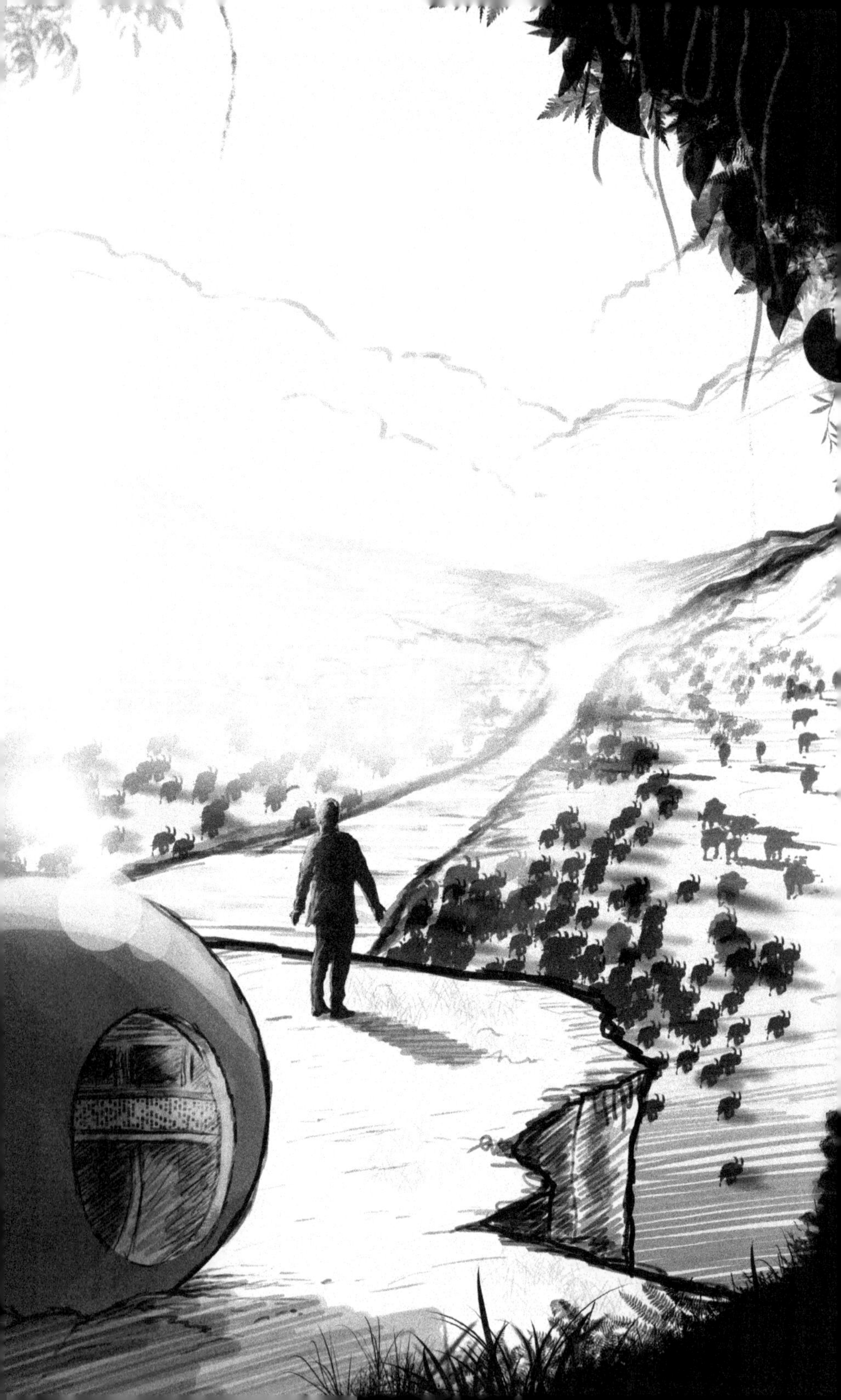

TimeMachineStory

Richmond A Clements

I admit it, building the time machine *was* a mistake. I know that now.

But… at the time. At the time, it had seemed like such a good idea. And when I had that idea, sitting there in the plane, looking out of the window, I couldn't wait to build it.

It had just come to me. I looked down at the city streets, criss crossing like the lines on a circuit board. The cars and people were pulses of information, moving from point to point on the board; it was all so clear. So I built the circuit board I had seen in the street plan, and constructed a time machine around it.

And it worked.

So now you've built a time machine – an honest to goodness working time machine – you've got some pretty major questions that you've got to ask yourself. Like where, or rather, when, would you go?

First moon landing? What about the first man on Mars? Woodstock? Gettysburg? Nuremberg?

No. If you are anything at all like me, you'll just stick to the classics. The birth of Christ, dinosaurs, the Rumble in the Jungle.

What can I tell you about these things?

I stepped into the time machine and back sixty million years. It was like stepping out of your car in the middle of a safari park.You know that bit in *Jurassic Park*? The bit where that Australian guy – can't remember his name – the guy in that hat, he looks down at a lake and all the different dinosaurs are drinking there? It was like that, only I was in the middle of it. There were so many of them. Thousands of animals the size of houses were lumbering around me. And the noise, the smell – it was like the stench of the elephant house in a zoo, only multiplied a thousand times. But the air was clean. Free from any hint of man's interference. So clean that you could smell it beneath the animal musk.

You know what comes next don't you?

Yeah, they started dying. It was my fault. Probably some virus or germ I carried along with me. What did I just say about man's interference..?

By hey! If I hadn't, then we wouldn't be here!

I thought long and hard about my next trip. I wanted to do something really useful to balance out the whole destroying an ecosystem thing. So, I finally decided on a quick jaunt into the future.

The future? Much as you would expect. Flying cars, giant insular city communities constructed in the middle of weather in turmoil and raised sea levels on a planet injured and scarred by brutal conflict.

Still, on the bright side, they have cool spaceships, moon bases and colonies on Mars. No aliens, unfortunately, but I probably hadn't gone far enough forward to meet any.

Anyway, back to the point. I found what I went to the future for, and brought it back with me. What had I gone looking for? The AIDS vaccine.

I decided to take it back to the early twentieth century and nip the disease in the bud.

Do you know what a vaccine is?

Put into simple terms, it is a small amount of the actual virus, enough to bolster the body's immune system. How was I to know that introducing a vaccine to a virus that did not yet exist would cause so much bother?

Look, I'm sorry. But at least we know there'll be cure in the end, eh?

At this point, you would be telling yourself that this time travel thing is a bad idea. Meddling with things that shouldn't be meddled with, that sort of thing. Not me. I put it down to bad luck, and figured third time lucky was the rule. Bad luck.

Maybe I should have said 'Bad timing'?

For a while after that, things got better, though it would be pointless for me to tell you what I achieved. When you think of it, any war I may have stopped, any disaster averted or assassination I foiled would, by definition, never have happened, so you wouldn't have heard of it.

No, I'm not stupid. I am now very wealthy, after my many successful investments, as well as a sizeable lottery jackpot. Okay, a few sizeable lottery jackpots. These I figured as payment for my many good deeds.

Maybe it was karma, but after the lottery wins, stuff started to go wrong.

I introduced Kurt Cobain to Courtney Love, John to Yoko, John to Ringo, Chas to Dave, Jack to Jackie. And to Marilyn. And a few others besides.

I told Barbara Cartland she looked good in pink.

What? The Kennedy assassination? Yeah, I know who did it. But trust me -

you do not want to know. You can see me in that film, by the way. I'm standing behind the guy with the umbrella.

But that's only the half of it. How do you live with the knowledge that you helped to split up the Beatles? Or worse, helped Wings stay together for an extra year?

How can a man come back from that? Can he redeem himself after suggesting to Abraham Lincoln that he needed a night out at the theatre?

After too many such incidents, I realised that my jaunts back and forth were causing more problems than they were solving.

Yes, I tried to put it right; went back to a few of my mistakes, but ended up making them worse. That's where the Kennedy thing comes in. The book depository window and the grassy knoll? Those were both me.. What a mess.

Kennedy, Lincoln, AIDS, Arch Duke Ferdinand and more. I killed a lot of people trying to do the right thing.

But how do I put all of *that* right?

It took me a while, but eventually, I arrived at the obvious answer. The solution was to stop myself before I built the thing.

But the application… when was the best time to stop myself?

I remember the exact moment that I had the idea. It seemed like yesterday; it seemed like a thousand years ago. It was probably both.

How do I stop myself?

I remember the exact moment. Looking down on the circuit board city. New York below me on September 11th.

How do I stop myself?

Richmond Clements is originally from N Ireland and now living in Northern Scotland. He is co-editor at *FutureQuake Press,* whose titles include the Eagle Award nominated *FutureQuake* and *2000AD* fanzine *Zarjaz.*
He has written numerous comic strips and the graphic novels *Turning Tiger, Ketsueki* and *Pirates of the Lost World.*

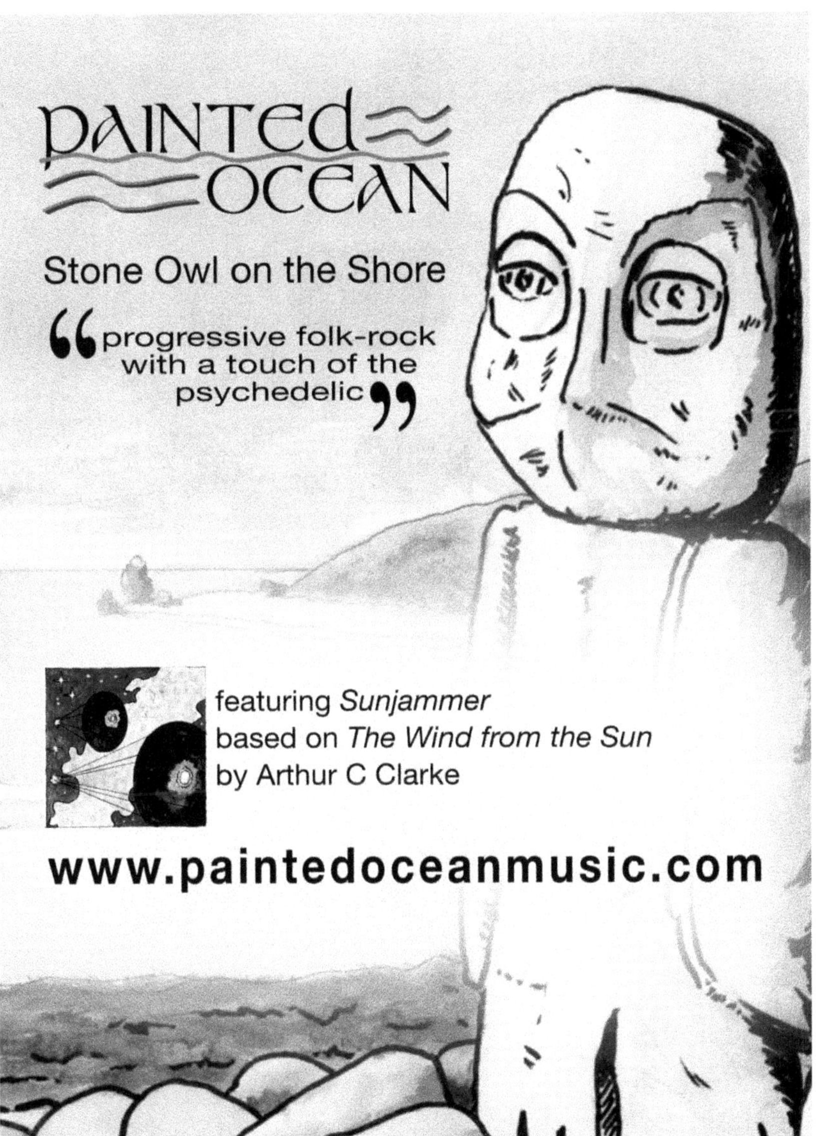
PAINTED OCEAN
Stone Owl on the Shore
"progressive folk-rock with a touch of the psychedelic"
featuring Sunjammer
based on The Wind from the Sun
by Arthur C Clarke
www.paintedoceanmusic.com

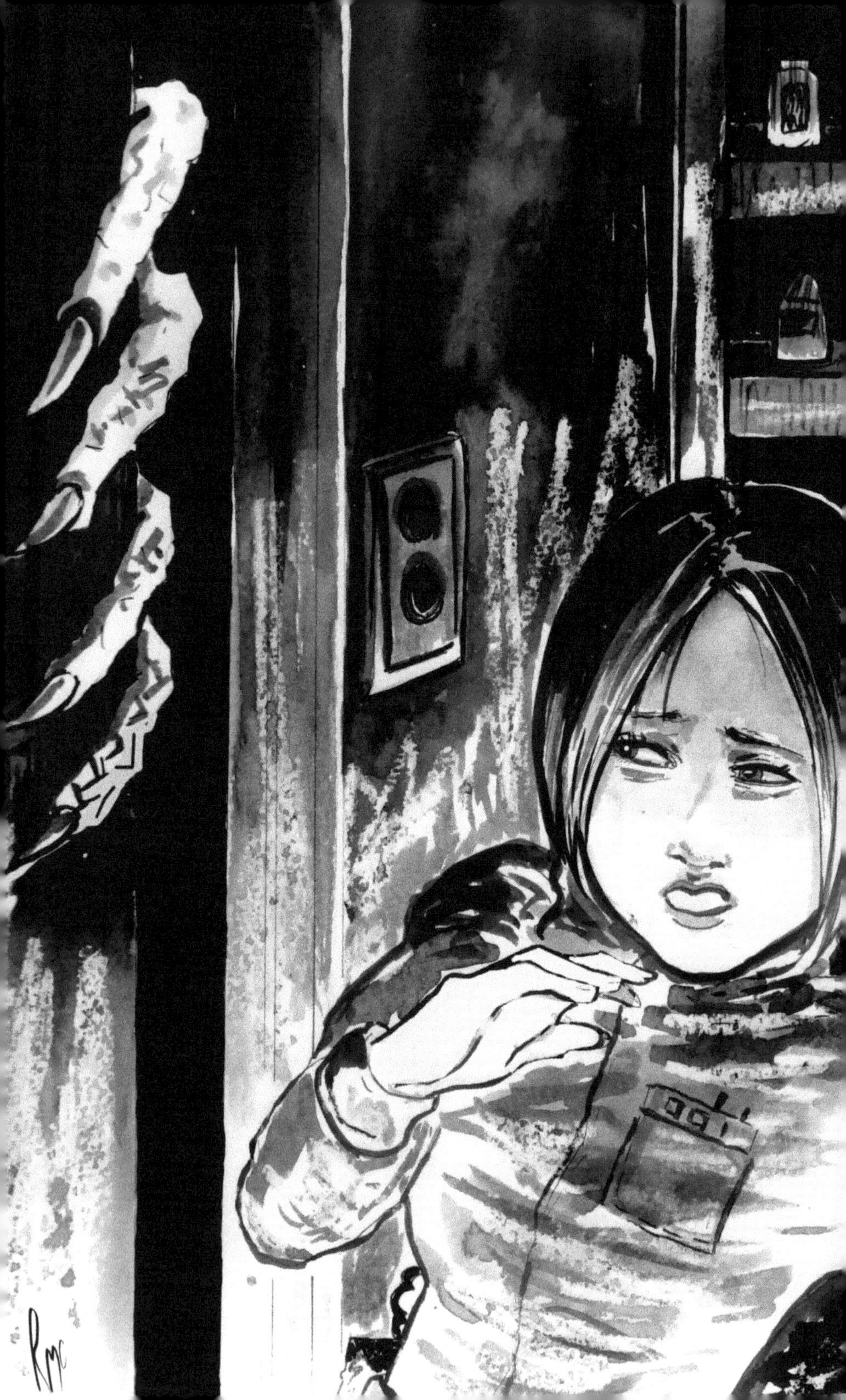

Cleanup on Deck 7

Claire Simpson

"Attention, all hands. We have an incursion on deck seven, starboard. I repeat, an incursion on deck seven, starboard. Initiate emergency procedures. Red alert."

Being on her first tour of duty, Janitor Grade One Nakata still had a tendency to get lost in the endless corridors of the *Lightspeed Warrior*. So when the announcement came over the comms she had to double-check the signs to see where she was. 'Deck 7: Starboard Aft'. Great.

What did the janitorial manual say about Arachnid incursions? Get back to base, stay out of the way, prepare for major clean-up operations afterwards. That was it. Seventeen pages about shifting unruly grease spots and nothing about what to do when a breach happened in front of you.

The growing shadows on the wall ahead were not the cavalry riding in to save her, judging by the shapes. Nakata dived blindly for the nearest door and hurled herself through, slapping at the button to close it behind her.

A store cupboard. Fantastic. She could never find the damn things when she needed them and now she was stuck in one. Better try to settle her breathing and hope they didn't figure out she was in here. "Nakata." The communicator at her waist crackled. Janitor Grade Two Dimitrov. "Report in, Nakata. Where are you?"

"Deck seven, starboard aft," she whispered, trying not to attract the attention of anything outside. "I can't really-"

"Say again, Nakata." Dimitrov didn't do quiet. "Where the hell are you?" Nakata lifted the communicator and spoke as loudly as she dared. "I'm in a cupboard on deck seven, starboard aft," she said. "There are hostiles right outside. I'll join you as soon as I'm-"

There was a sudden screech, claws scraping down the outside of the door. They'd found her.

"Did you say a cupboard?" barked Dimitrov.

"Be quiet," Nakata snapped. "There's one right outside the door. If you want to be useful, get a squad from Military down here."

The noise from outside was setting her teeth on edge. Nakata shut off her communicator (technically a class five offence, but that only mattered if she survived) and put her hands over her ears. If she was lucky, someone would come to clear out this section before the monster out there figured out how to open the door.

There was a jaunty bing and the door began to slide open. Nakata dived for the button on her side to close it, but a massive clawed hand caught the edge of the door and forced it open.

She'd seen 'Racks on news reports, and in training videos, but nothing quite compared to having one towering over her in the flesh. It was forcing itself through the doorway, teeth and razor-sharp claws advancing while the grotesque bulk of its abdomen stayed out in the corridor. Nakata shrank into the furthest corner, though she couldn't escape its reach. The rancid stench of slime and death clogged her lungs.

This was it then. Janitor Grade One Nakata, tragically killed in action during the first incursion of her first tour of duty. Another statistic in the unending war, mourned only by the brother she'd left planetside. Another piece of paperwork for Dimitrov to bitch about.

As the creature studied her with compound eyes, some desperate survival instinct kicked in and Nakata grabbed the only weapon she could use from one of the shelves, pointed it at the beast and squeezed the trigger.

The bottle of Shini-Brite gave a pathetic squeak as it squirted a thin stream of liquid in the monster's face.

There was a single moment of stillness, during which Nakata closed her eyes and accepted her fate. There was a hiss and an almighty shrieking.

The liquid was fizzing where it had touched the 'Rack, the powerful grease-cutting action working overtime on the alien slime and burning through the skin beneath. The monster was clawing at its own face, trying to clear the froth away. Nakata gave another experimental squirt and it shrieked louder, scrabbling backwards out of the door, leaving behind the fresh scent of pine.

One corner of Nakata's mouth lifted in a smile. There were plenty of bottles in here, so she grabbed several and jammed them into her belt before taking one in each hand. Then she stepped daintily through the door, giving the writhing mess in the corridor one last squirt for luck.

It was time to get back to work.

Claire Simpson writes code by day and stories by night (or at least that's what she claims to be doing when she's actually on Twitter). Congenitally incapable of doing nothing, she also sews, crochets and favours a peaty single malt if you're buying.

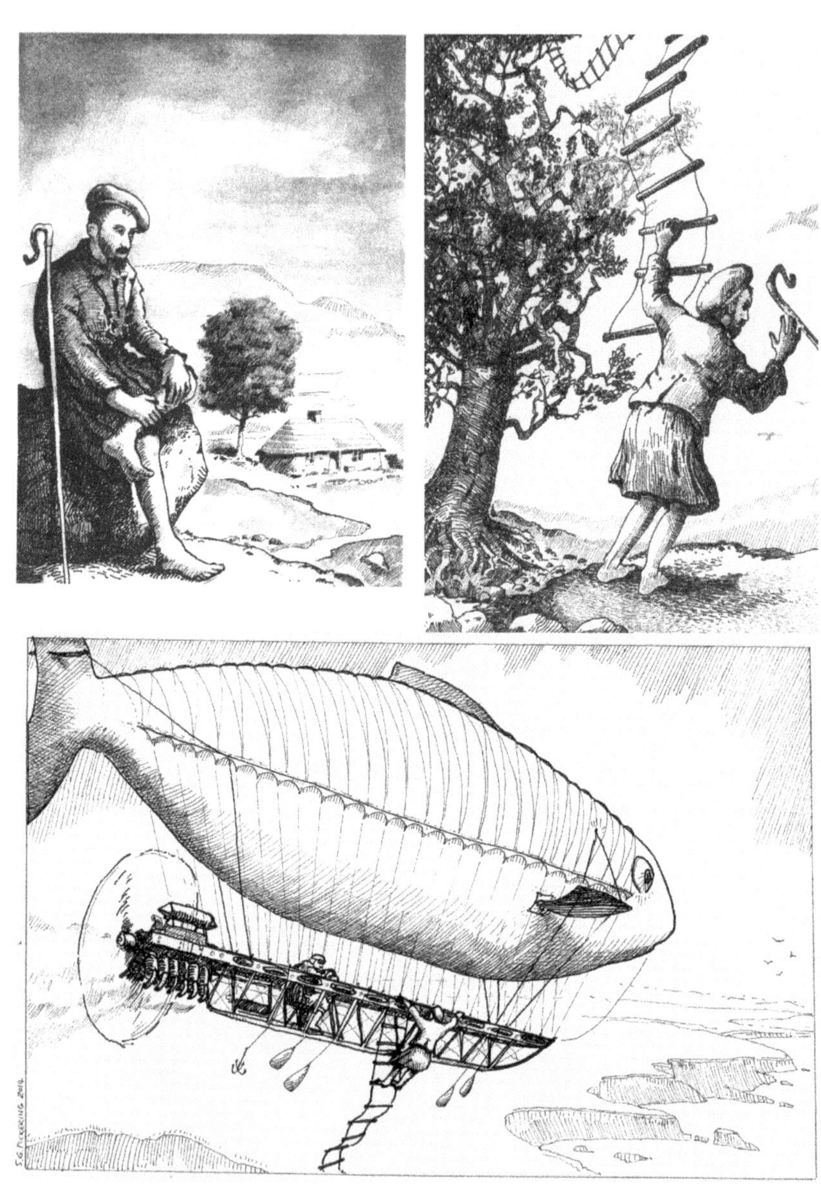

Story Competition Number 1

Story Competition

Sharpen your bluetooth-enabled iquill and dip into your jar of ink made from finest Jovian squid. On the facing page we've a specially commissioned artwork from Dumfries artist Stephen Pickering, and we'd like you to write a science fiction story inspired by one or more of the panels.

The prize for the best story is £80, a print of Stephen's artwork and a 4 issue digital subscription to *Shoreline of Infinity*. The story will be published in Issue 3, of which the winner will also receive a printed edition. We'll also do an interview with the winning author to run alongside the story.

Maximum word count: 4,000 words.
To submit your story please do so via the website at www.shorelineofinfinity.com
The deadline is midnight UK time (GMT) of 21st December 2015.

Interview: Charles Stross

Charles Stross is one of Britain's best and most prolific science fiction writers. He emerged in the 1980s as a short story writer appearing in *Interzone*. Apparently he could often be seen at SF conventions wandering around with a half-finished manuscript under his arm. His talent and persistence paid off; his first novel, *Singularity Sky*, was published in 2003 and nominated for a Hugo the year after. He has since released a whole string of books, each one stuffed with fizzing ideas, strong characters and an I-dare-you-not-to-turn-the-page attitude. We welcome Charlie to our first issue of Shoreline of Infinity.

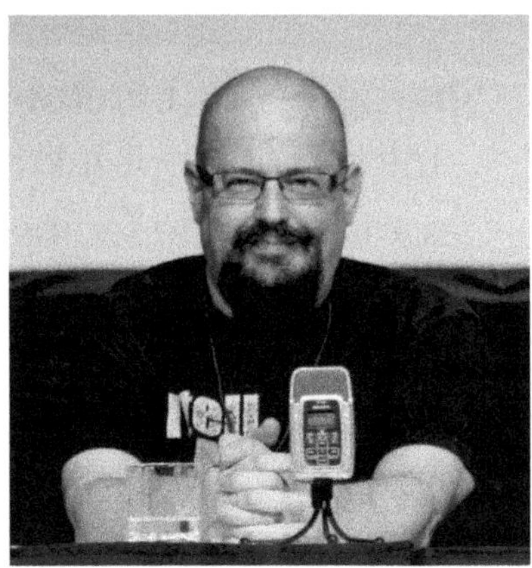

Shoreline of Infinity: When and how did you first realise you were a writer? What influenced you and what drew you to SF?

Charles Stross: I'm not sure when I began writing. Certainly, one of my earliest memories was of my mother sitting at the kitchen table, hammering away on a manual typewriter, trying to write a novel. I think she only got about two chapters done—but somehow this imprinted on me the idea that books were written by people, and it was okay to write fiction.

Around age twelve I got an English teacher who set my class a fiction-writing project, to fill an entire exercise book with a story over the course of a term: I was one of the 10% who filled two books. At that time, the mid-to-late 1970s, Dungeons and Dragons was catching on in the UK and I was playing with friends. I borrowed the portable typewriter my sister'd learned to type on for writing up D&D adventure scenarios, taught myself to type, then somehow slid into writing fiction around the age of 14 or 15.

This was in the late 1970s to early 1980s. We made our own entertainment back then: we had 3 channels of TV in black and white, no VCR (let alone DVDs), no internet, no computers. On the other hand, I grew up surrounded by books ...

I never really thought about writing anything *other than* science fiction or fantasy. It was what I grew up reading, because it held my interest—remember, we're talking teenaged males here. And what I wrote was pretty dire until I hit my twenties, much as you'd expect: the real function of literature is to explore the human condition through creative but plausible lies, and you can't really do that until you've acquired at least a minimal grip on what the human condition is. SF and Fantasy offer the broader context of letting us examine how the human condition might be modified by—in the case of SF—possible but not actually existent circumstances, and in the face of fantasy, by frankly implausible conditions that nevertheless have emotional (or mythic) resonance.

Together these genre categories belong to what critic John Clute labels the fantastika—that branch of literature that diverges from the ultra-mundane path that so much mainstream literary fiction took during the 20th century.

It's worth bearing in mind that one of the functions of fiction is play. Much as playful activities provide young mammals with an opportunity to rehearse useful adult behaviours—if you've ever seen kittens or puppies play-fighting, there's a big clue—fiction provides us, even as adults, with an opportunity to rehearse situations we've never experienced.

"It's worth bearing in mind that one of the functions of fiction is play."

The trouble I had with the realist mainstream branch of literature when I was young was that it was rehearsing stuff that didn't resonate with my life. You don't have to live an adventure-filled life, hob-nob with aliens, or spend time in a haunted dungeon, to feel that a form of literature that barely admits the existence of the technological sphere—much less of any technology more abstruse than the television, telephone, or automobile—is somehow missing key aspects of how we live.

Let me give you a concrete example. Since I turned 18, our computers have grown in performance roughly a billion-fold, and we all think nothing these days of carrying around magic mirrors that give us access to the sum total of human knowledge at a finger's touch. We use them for watching cute animal videos and for taking photographs of ourselves. One side-effect of this technology is that our governments spy on us in a manner that would have warmed the chilly hearts of any pre-1970s dictatorship's secret police. Another is that we're living through the most photographed time in human history, with about 20% of all photographs ever taken having been snapped in the past year, and 30-40% of *them* being uploaded to Facebook, which in turn has a few million computers permanently tasked with recognizing and tagging faces in those photographs, working out where they were taken and what this says about our physical social relationships ... and then using this insanely hypertrophied police state infrastructure to market consumer goods at us.

So we're under Gestapo-on-steroids level surveillance all the time, through automated snitches that we *pay* for the privilege of carrying, and the main subjective consequence of this is that if we're seen frequently with someone who just died, we get ads for wreaths and condolences cards.

SF gives me a tool for working through those issues, and in particular through the consequences of the third industrial revolution that I've lived through. The traditional literary realist-mode novel doesn't do that. Most novelists don't really get a start until they're in their thirties (it's that human condition thing, again: you have to have some experience of life before you can write about it), and by the time they're into their second decade of writing they're middle-aged—the typical point at which engaging with change becomes difficult. If they spent their youth acquiring a pure liberal arts education, then they almost certainly missed out on the quantitative sciences and the engineering arts—and so they won't be a very reliable guide to the world in flux around us.

Your first story, The Boys, was published in 1987 in *Interzone*. That, dare I say, is looking back nearly 30 years. Before that was the 'Golden Age' of SF in the 40s and early 50s, with writers such as Asimov, Bradbury, Clarke, Heinlein and pals. How would you compare being a Science Fiction writer in those earlier days, to when you started out, and for anyone new to writing SF today?

CS: I have no idea how to compare being an SF writer today with the 1980s, because the changes wrought by the arrival of the internet have been so pervasive and insidious that it's hard to remember what things were like back then.

"I find the human dimension of storytelling increasingly important as I grow older."

Circa 1982, roughly 40 SF/F novels were published in the UK per year, and one magazine (*Interzone*) was regularly buying and publishing short stories. Unless you lived near a town with a specialist bookshop who could buy grey-market imports from the USA, that was it. Much like trying to explain the era of two television channels in black and white to someone reared on cable TV and YouTube, it's very hard to think yourself back into what it was like in those days.

We've seen such a massive flowering of written and visual media in our field that it's hard to remember that it was a mostly-ignored ghetto back then; today geek culture is mainstream. A third of Hollywood's movie output is tailored to the public appetite for SF/F; Dr Who is one of the BBC's most watched TV shows by adults: if you turn on the TV and watch the adverts, you'll rapidly see that around 80-90% of them employ computer-generated graphics and generally use them to portray impossibilities—often relying on *SFnal* imagery. While rhetorical devices ("that's really science fictional, isn't it?") are part of the language of the TV or radio commentator or newspaper columnist, the reality is that we're living in a science fictional age. We don't have jet packs, food pills, or holidays on the moon, but we have 250mph atomic-powered trains (or at least the French do), sushi on every street corner, and the pocket-sized magic mirrors that connect us to the sum total of human knowledge.

One side-effect of this is that the markets for fiction are evolving furiously fast. We tend to forget that, although people have been experimenting with ebooks since the mid-1980s, the commercial market for them was less than 1% of all book sales as recently as 2009. (Today, 50% of my book sales are in electronic form.) Any advice I received when I was starting out is long since obsolete; any advice I could offer to a new writer starting out today will be of similarly questionable utility.

You said in an interview in *Revolution SF* "the core study of any branch of fiction is people." I've just finished reading your latest Laundry Files book *The Rhesus Chart* and it's been a pleasure to watch Bob Howard mature and grow throughout the series.

How important to you is getting the human perspective of your ideas and story across to your readers? Maybe it's

time for other SF writers to focus a lot more on how people react and respond to our "Sfnal" world?

CS: I find the human dimension of storytelling increasingly important as I grow older. We're living, as I said earlier, in the science fictional future of the 20th century: if you want a mere sense-of-wonder kick and the weirdness of the cosmos or the elaboration of our technosphere you don't need to read fiction for that—you can get it in the pages of *New Scientist* every week, or in the newspapers.

"...we aren't about naively predicting the future: rather, we're about figuring out what human beings will make of the future."

To the extent that relevance is important to written SF (and I'd be the last person to deny that you don't need relevance for recreational escapism, which is and traditionally has been about 80-90% of our genre's raison d'etre), we aren't about naively predicting the future: rather, we're about figuring out what human beings will make of the future. (While it's possible to write SF that features no human beings at all—in settings where humanity never existed, or is extinct—it's hard work, and it's a niche market.)

Fiction is a ritualized rehearsal for life, so fiction in future settings that asks questions like "what is it going to be like to live in a world where everyone is on the internet 24x7 via their clothing and the artefacts in their environment" may be useful. Deeper questions like, "what happens when the sort of people who run fake Microsoft Support call centres to install RATs [Remote Access Trojans] on the PCs of pensioners in order to steal their bank details discover the Internet Of Things" can provide lots of material for stories of unanticipated consequences and humanity.

A lot of this stuff is deeply weird, because the way we're embodying crude representations of our own intelligence in the artefacts around us echoes the paranoid, strange realm of a Philip K. Dick novel—advertisements that crawl cockroach-like into our cars or living rooms and shout at us, doorknobs that won't let us out of our home until we pay a subscription fee in accordance with an arcane contract we don't remember signing. And these representations of our intellect are deeply broken insofar as they're inflexible and they model human modes of behaviour and cognition only partially. For example, consider Facebook's attempt at giving everyone an annual album of their uploaded photographs from the past year, sorted by "popularity" (how many people "liked" the photos or tagged them). Obviously this seemed like a good idea to the bright twenty-something engineers who came up with the idea: it never occurred to them to put themselves in the shoes of a grieving parent whose only child had died of leukaemia over the preceding year, precipitating a divorce, because *of course* they and their friends never upload photographs to Facebook that are associated with sad or unhappy memories.

There's going to be a lot more of this sort of weird emotional brokenness in our superficially-smart future. And that's before we get into big current topics like climate change, the ageing of the global population, the fallout from the financialization and asset stripping of the west, and so on.

I'm going to ask this even though it's just a few weeks before the General Election in the UK, with the whole thing up in the air and feeling balanced on the edge of uncertainty. How much would you agree with Arthur C Clarke's 1970 comment when he said "Politicians should read science fiction not westerns and detective stories," and what lessons can the politicians learn?

CS: ACC was right; unfortunately someone was reading him, and that someone was Rupert Murdoch (who used to phone up Clarke for a chat every week, or so I'm told). Murdoch got the message about satellite TV broadcasting and its utility in spreading a political agenda; since then, all the politicians have been living with the fallout of Clarke's nostrum.

Politicians these days are mostly career professionals. To get to the top while still young enough to be viable as a prime ministerial candidate precludes any experience of the world outside of politics. This is, I think, a disaster for us in the long term because we've handed over our government to managerialists like Ed Milliband and public relations guys like David Cameron. They're non-specialists who are at the mercy of lobbyists funded by the industries and economic sectors they're supposed to control. These in turn are largely run by big public corporations. The joint stock corporation is essentially a form of very slow artificial intelligence that we invented about 300 years ago: these days they are increasingly replacing their executive and decision making functions with automated but not individually intelligent units. So our politicians are out in front, pretending to lead—but in reality they're being steered from behind by not-terribly-bright sociopathic AIs fine-tuned for short-term survival and profitability at any cost.

How we get out of this mess is not obvious, but I doubt the eventual solution will emerge from within our existing political framework.

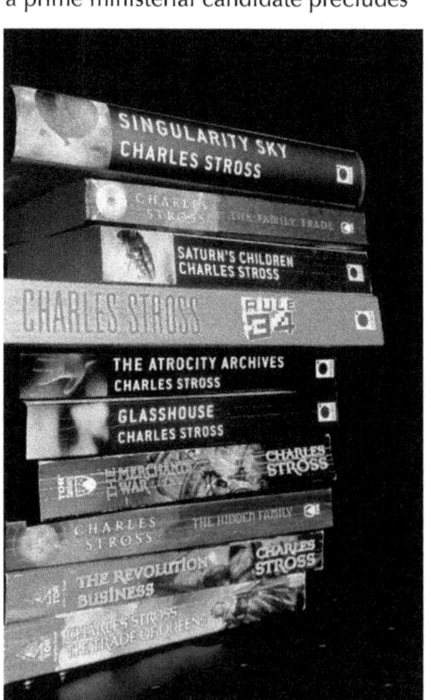

What can we look forward to seeing you publishing in the new few months or so?

CS: I've got a new novel coming out on July 7th, from Orbit (in the UK; in the USA it's published by Ace). It's "The Annihilation Score", and it's book six in the Laundry Files series. Unlike earlier Laundry novels, this one breaks with Bob, hitherto our sole narrator and first-person viewpoint—it's told by Dr Mo O'Brien, who is parachuted into the Home Office to deal with an emergency: a plague of superheroes. And supervillains ...

Charles Stross, many thanks for taking the time out to talk to Shoreline of Infinity.

Border Crossings

Steve Green

Steve is a stalwart of Science Fiction fandom, starting out way back in the 1970s. He is well known on the SF Convention circuit and was Chair of Novacon 2014. He is a freelance editor and journalist and has brought his skills to bear in many SF publications. We welcome Steve as our first regular columnist.

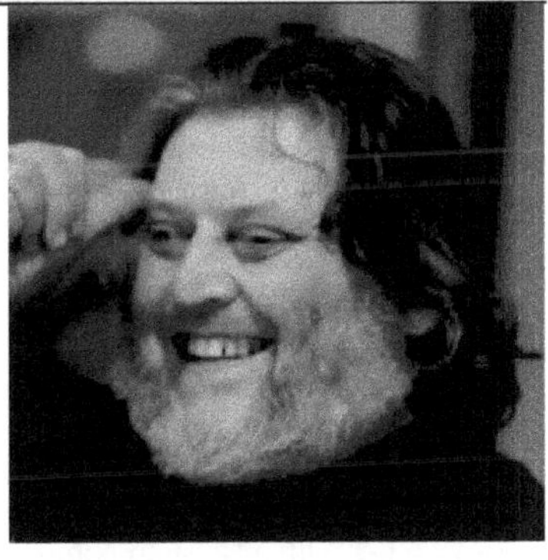

I first stepped upon Scottish soil exactly thirty-five years ago, appropriately enough to attend the first National British Science Fiction Convention held north of Hadrian's Wall. It was a dismally cold and miserable April weekend, and Glasgow's Albany Hotel was playing host to hundreds of English sf fans who may well have considered travelling to the lunar surface less of a voyage into the unknown (my oldest friend and I had spent the first five hours of Good Friday crammed into a not-so-good railway carriage, chatting to the alleged brother of the leader of our destination city's Hell's Angels chapter, with only the prospect of the Albany bar serving Belhaven 80/- at 47p a pint to buoy up our spirits).

What I didn't know then, as we emerged into the damp air and politely declined our erstwhile fellow traveller's offer to go wake up a local publican (with a gentle shake, should it prove necessary) so the three of us could launch the bank holiday weekend properly (these being the days before sensible Easter opening hours, when the only way to get truly crucified was to nail the lead role in a passion play), was that the acclaimed French film director Bertrand Tavernier had walked down those same rain-drenched avenues just a few months earlier, having found the perfect setting for a very bleak and disturbingly prescient socio-political augury.

Dangerous Visions

Tavernier's inspiration for his new project Death Watch (aka La mort en direct) was David Compton's 1973 novel The Continuous Katherine Mortenhoe (edited for US readers as The Unsleeping Eye), another of the author's explorations of moral dilemmas within a near-future context and one which echoes his 1968 breakthrough Synthajoy, wherein human experience becomes a transferable product, rather in the manner of such movies as The Sorcerers (1967), Brainstorm (1983) and Strange Days (1995).

Despite Mortenhoe appearing the same year as PBS' landmark documentary series An American Family, now judged by many as Patient Zero in the current plague of 'reality television' formats, it's unlikely Compton (then living in London) could have been influenced to any degree as he conceived a society so utterly devoid of colour its worker ants must draw succour from the more damaged and distressed within their midst.

Sydney Pollack's regular collaborator of choice, Daniel Rayfiel, had come on board to co-author the script with Tavernier, a relationship which would later produce the Oscar-winning Dexter Gordon biopic Round Midnight (1986). Together, they took Compton's dark, decaying panorama and embued it with harsh realism, the director having decided early on to eschew the comfortably sterile imagery of such technophilic movies as Things to Come (1936) and Logan's Run (1976) in favour of a grim, grey urban wasteland. Glasgow City Council's "Smiles Better" advertising hoardings clearly failed to persuade Tavernier he hadn't located the ideal candidate.

Their storyline in large part revolves around the smart, sensitive author Katherine Mortenhoe, already adrift in a world which prefers computer-crafted pabulum to works of genuine literature. Hers is a Britain virtually cleansed of disease, but filthy with poverty and despair, poised at the tipping point towards total collapse. Mortenhoe's unique diagnosis of a terminal, incurable illness offers certain more shadowy elements – a sinister fusion of Westminster and media – to approach her with a Faustian compact: in return for hefty remuneration, she will spend her final days in the unblinking gaze of 24/7 voyeurism. Bread and circuses moulded from wafers and last rites, for an audience no longer capable of grasping the truth of death.

Enter cracked lensman Roddy, estranged from his partner and so desperate for a new anchor in this sea of troubles that he agrees to have video cameras implanted into his eyes, allowing his employers to spy upon Katherine regardless of her refusal to comply with State-sanctioned surveillance. The catch? Prolonged darkness will lead to permanent blindness.

Thus the drama, thus the horror: she runs, he follows and the moronic masses spectate in silence, enraptured by their television screens whilst all around falls into dust and chaos.

On this high-definition microscope slide, the trivial gathers absurd import: in what could almost be a trail for the next season of Big Brother, or perhaps a summing up of this culture's entire Facebook / Twitter / Instagram / MeGeneration descent into narcissistic entropy, Katherine observes, "Everything's of interest, but nothing matters."

Death Watch (1980): directed by Bertrand Tavernier; screenplay by Betrand Tavernier and Daniel Rayfiel; based upon the novel The Continuous Katherine Mortenhoe, written by D G Compton. Featuring Romy Schneider as Katherine Mortenhoe, Harvey Keitel as Roddy, Harry Dean Stanton as Vincent Ferriman, Max von Sydow as Gerald Mortenhoe; Thérèse Liotard as Tracy. Released on Blu-ray in 2012 by Park Circus.

Under the Skin (2013): directed by Jonathan Glazer; screenplay by Walter Campbell and Jonathan Glazer; based upon the novel Under the Skin by Michel Faber. Featuring Scarlett Johansson, Jeremy McWilliams, Michael Moreland, Dave Acton. Released on Blu-ray in 2014 by StudioCanal.

First held in 1948, the National British Science Fiction (aka Eastercon) returned to Scotland in 1983, 1986, 1991, 2000, 2006 and 2014. All six were held in Glasgow, which also hosted the World Science Fiction Convention in 1995 and 2005. Next year's Eastercon will be held in Manchester.

Loving the Alien

Tavernier's success in second-guessing the futurescape bore bitter fruit: instead of the gleaming spires and plastic domes which now look as ill-imagined as food pills and hovercars, most cities stumbled onwards with few obvious changes beyond the introduction of smoking bans in pubs, high street off-licences (not all bad, then) and – in a near-nod to Compton's dystopian fatalism – the highest CCTV count per capita in

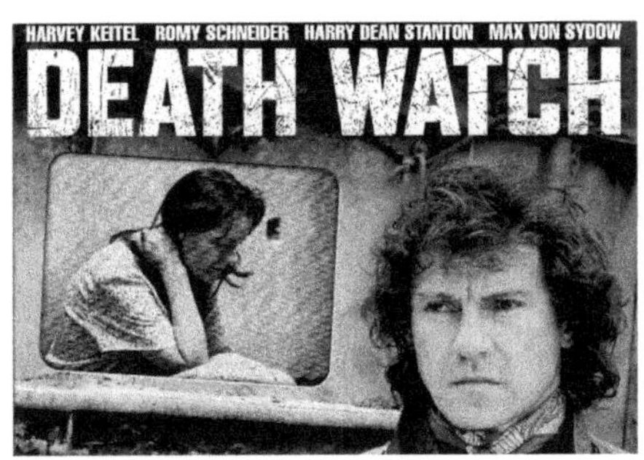

Europe. No fewer than thirty-two years might have passed before Jonathan Glazer arrived in Glasgow to direct his third movie, but you'd be hard-pressed to spot the join.

Michel Faber's Whitbread-winning source novel had appeared in 2000, the same year as Glazer's debut feature Sexy Beast, but the film-maker soon realised its route would be as long and circuitous as the highland byways Faber's predatory extraterrestrials prowl for unwary hitch-hikers. At various points over the following decade, both Brad Pitt and Gemma Arteton were attached to the project, until Glazer and his co-writer Walter Campbell decided to shift the opening two-thirds of their storyline into an urban setting and downsize the main cast to a single, female alien.

Faber, no stranger to cultural dislocation (born in Holland and educated in Australia before making Scotland his home in 1993), had used his novel to explore themes of self, sexuality and isolation. Clearly, Glazer needed to somehow find an actress with enough box office clout to provide Under the Skin with some long-overdue traction, but one able to slip unrecognised into the pedestrian traffic passing through a Glasgow shopping centre. I'm certain I wasn't the only person left fairly surprised when this chimera turned out to be Hollywood headliner Scarlett Johansson.

It's our own fault, of course, for buying into the baloney studio press offices extrude whenever she turns up in a 'blockbuster' action thriller such as the recent Avengers: Age of Ultron. In actuality, Ms Johansson has an admirable history of appearing in her industry's equivalent of off-Broadway productions, ranging from historical dramas (Girl With a Pearl Earring, The Other Boleyn Girl) through romantic comedy (Match Point, He's Just Not That Into You) to fantasy (The Prestige, Lucy) and the delightfully odd (Ghost World, Her); clearly, a young woman who enjoys a challenge.

The fact that we never learn her character's true name ('Isserley' in the novel) is perfectly in tune with the shroud of invisibility Ms Johansson dons as she strolls into the Buchanan Galleries or encounters a well-lubricated hen party outside a Livingston nightclub. It's a deeply thoughtful and considered performance, possibly nuanced by her knowledge that she is truly alien to this environment, hiding her own identity just as the quasi-female extraterrestrial must simulate humanity in order to complete its mission.

Glazer's use of hidden cameras – as many as ten running simultaneously – during his star's improvised interactions with unsuspecting non-actors adds an extra level of disconnect to this film's already dreamlike narrative, as well as ironically echoing Compton's predictions nearly four decades earlier. That's the way with the future: it's just like the present, only more so.

Bet you can't still get Belhaven 80/- at 47p a pint, though.

Steve Green is a freelance editor and journalist who first met *Shoreline of Infinity's* Noel Chidwick in 1977, when they launched a science fiction fanzine. *Plus ça change.*

SF Caledonia

John Buchan: SF Writer?

Paul F Cockburn

Despite numerous accomplishments in his lifetime – as a publisher, historian, politician and statesman – John Buchan (1875 - 1940) is chiefly remembered now as the author of *The Thirty-Nine Steps* (1915). Usefully, in an introductory note to the now-classic espionage-thriller, Buchan explained his goal of delivering a story "where the incidents defy the probabilities and march just inside the borders of the possible". Raymond Chandler once declared that to be the perfect formula for a thriller; arguably, it's also an apt definition for the most successful supernatural stories.

Buchan had always been attracted to old legends and secret places, whether in the Scottish Borders of his early childhood, the wilderness of Southern Africa, or the rolling Oxfordshire countryside in which he later settled. Buchan's lifelong fascination with the mysterious, uncanny and inexplicable is most obviously seen in his many overtly supernatural short stories, but even his novels repeatedly reflect a core belief in the underlying fragility of our civilisation, and of other realities lurking in the chaos beyond.

"You think that a wall as solid as the earth separates civilisation from barbarism. I tell you the division is a thread, a sheet of glass. A touch here, a push there, and you bring back the reign of Saturn." Those words may have been put in the mouth of the principal villain of *The Power-Room* (1916) but the concept they describe echoes across most of Buchan's fiction.

It's a particularly brutish barbarism, for example, which we're shown in "No-Man's Land" (1899), in which an Oxford scholar discovers Ancient Picts living underneath some remote Scottish hills. Yet, keeping within those "borders of the possible", Buchan ensures that their survival isn't down to some fantastical device. His university education (first at Glasgow, then Oxford) may have been in the classics, but he was interested in the latest scientific ideas of his time: and, by implication, that meant writing what the American editor and scholar Everett F Bleiler described as "an early example of Science Fiction".

Which brings us to *Space*. First published in May 1911, the story may now appear somewhat convoluted in its telling, but when you consider the quality of the prose and its core idea of strange and desolate alien dimensions barely glimpsed through mathematics, then it isn't just among the purest examples of Buchan's writing you can possibly read. It's also, surprisingly perhaps, pure Science Fiction!

Paul F Cockburn is a freelance magazine journalist specialising in arts & culture, equality issues, and popular science. Self-declared child of the Space Age, excited by science fiction from early childhood—he blames The Clangers, really. As far as this 21st century is concerned, would probably not swap his iPad for a jet-pack.

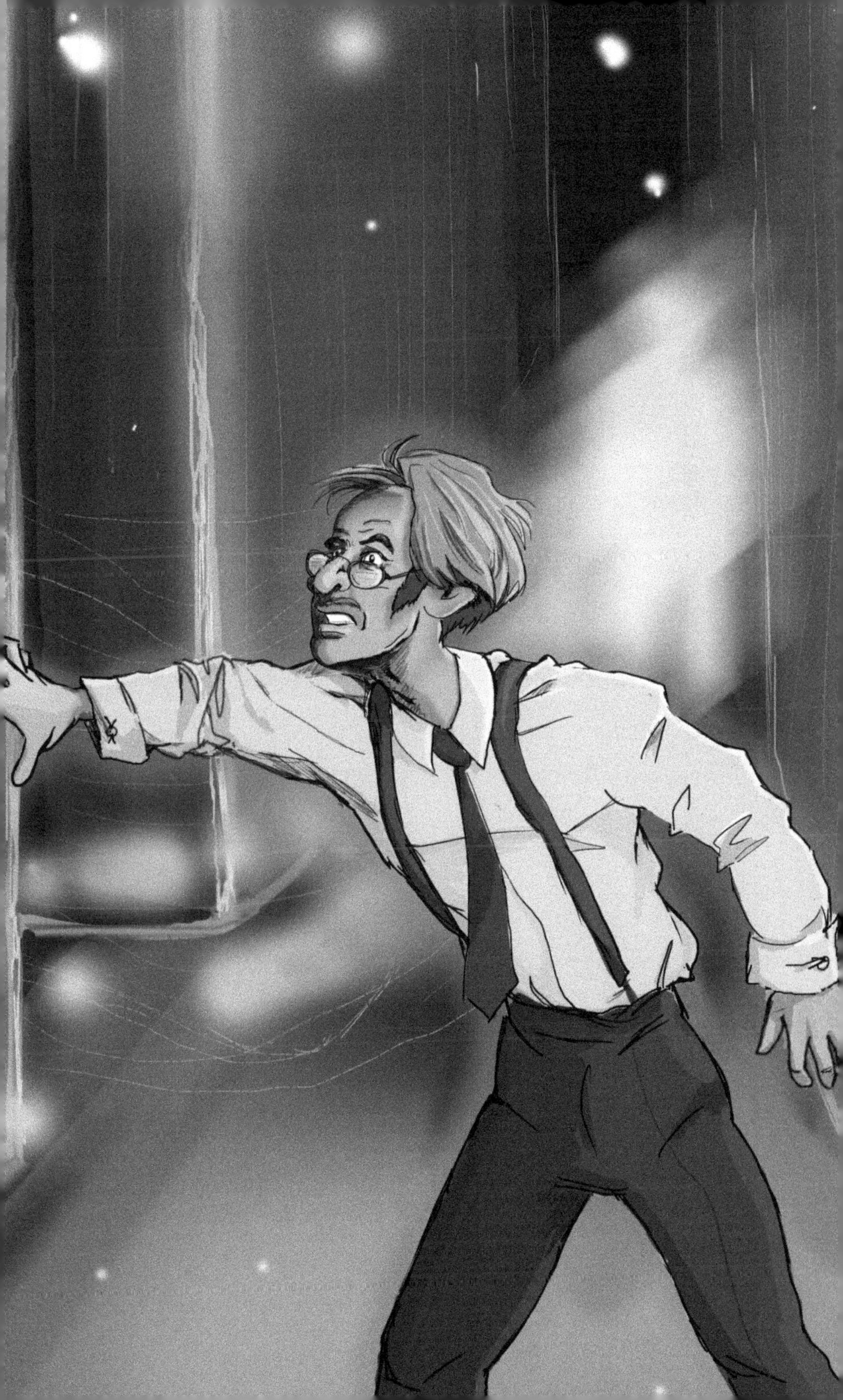

Space

John Buchan

Leithen told me this story one evening in early September as we sat beside the pony track which gropes its way from Glenvalin up the Correi na Sidhe. I had arrived that afternoon from the south, while he had been taking an off-day from a week's stalking, so we had walked up the glen together after tea to get the news of the forest. A rifle was out on the Correi na Sidhe beat, and a thin spire of smoke had risen from the top of Sgurr Dearg to show that a stag had been killed at the burnhead. The lumpish hill pony with its deer-saddle had gone up the Correi in a gillie's charge while we followed at leisure, picking our way among the loose granite rocks and the patches of wet bogland. The track climbed high on one of the ridges of Sgurr Dearg, till it hung over a caldron of green glen with the Alt-na-Sidhe churning in its linn a thousand feet below. It was a breathless evening, I remember, with a pale-blue sky just clearing from the haze of the day. West-wind weather may make the North, even in September, no bad imitation of the Tropics, and I sincerely pitied the man who all these stifling hours had been toiling on the screes of Sgurr Dearg. By-and-by we sat down on a bank of heather, and idly watched the trough swimming at our feet. The clatter of the pony's hoofs grew fainter, the drone of bees had gone, even the midges seemed to have forgotten their calling. No place on earth can be so deathly still as a deer-forest early in the season before the stags have begun roaring, for there are no sheep with their homely noises, and only the rare croak of a raven breaks the silence. The hillside was far from sheer-one could have walked down with a little care-but something in the shape of the hollow and the remote gleam of white water gave it an extraordinary depth and space. There was a shimmer left from the day's heat, which invested bracken and rock and scree with a curious airy unreality. One could almost have believed that the eye had tricked the mind, that all was mirage, that five yards from the path the solid earth fell away into nothingness. I have a bad head, and instinctively I drew farther back into the heather. Leithen's eyes were looking vacantly before him.

"Did you ever know Hollond?" he asked.

Then he laughed shortly. "I don't know why I asked that, but somehow this place reminded me of Hollond. That glimmering hollow looks as if it were the beginning of eternity. It must be eerie to live with the feeling always on one."

Leithen seemed disinclined for further exercise. He lit a pipe and smoked quietly for a little. "Odd that you didn't know Hollond. You must have heard his name. I thought you amused yourself with metaphysics."

Then I remembered. There had been an erratic genius who had written some articles in Mind on that dreary subject, the mathematical conception of infinity. Men had praised them to me, but I confess I never quite understood their argument. "Wasn't he some sort of mathematical professor?" I asked.

"He was, and, in his own way, a tremendous swell. He wrote a book on Number which has translations in every European language. He is dead now, and the Royal Society founded a medal in his honour. But I wasn't thinking of that side of him."

It was the time and place for a story, for the pony would not be back for an hour. So I asked Leithen about the other side of Hollond which was recalled to him by Correi na Sidhe. He seemed a little unwilling to speak...

"I wonder if you will understand it. You ought to, of course, better than me, for you know something of philosophy. But it took me a long time to get the hang of it, and I can't give you any kind of explanation. He was my fag at Eton, and when I began to get on at the Bar I was able to advise him on one or two private matters, so that he rather fancied my legal ability. He came to me with his story because he had to tell someone, and he wouldn't trust a colleague. He said he didn't want a scientist to know, for scientists were either pledged to their own theories and wouldn't understand, or, if they understood, would get ahead of him in his researches. He wanted a lawyer, he said, who was accustomed to weighing evidence. That was good sense, for evidence must always be judged by the same laws, and I suppose in the long-run the most abstruse business comes down to a fairly simple deduction from certain data. Anyhow, that was the way he used to talk, and I listened to him, for I liked the man, and had an enormous respect for his brains. At Eton he sluiced down all the mathematics they could give him, and he was an astonishing swell at Cambridge. He was a simple fellow, too, and talked no more jargon than he could help. I used to climb with him in the Alps now and then, and you would never have guessed that he had any thoughts beyond getting up steep rocks.

"It was at Chamonix, I remember, that I first got a hint of the matter that was filling his mind. We had been taking an off-day, and were sitting in the hotel garden, watching the Aiguilles getting purple in the twilight. Chamonix always makes me choke a little-it is so crushed in by those great snow masses. I said something about it—said I liked the open spaces like the Gornegrat or the Bel Alp better. He asked me why: if it was the difference of the air, or merely the wider horizon? I said it was the sense of not being crowded, of living in an empty world. He repeated the word 'empty' and laughed.

"'By "empty" you mean,' he said, 'where things don't knock up against you?'

I told him No. I mean just empty, void, nothing but blank aether.

"You don't knock up against things here, and the air is as good as you want. It can't be the lack of ordinary emptiness you feel."

"I agreed that the word needed explaining. 'I suppose it is mental restlessness,' I said. 'I like to feel that for a tremendous distance there is nothing round me. Why, I don't know. Some men are built the other way and have a terror of space.'

"He said that that was better. 'It is a personal fancy, and depends on your KNOWING that there is nothing between you and the top of the Dent Blanche. And you know because your eyes tell you there is nothing. Even if you were blind, you might have a sort of sense about adjacent matter. Blind men often have it. But in any case, whether got from instinct or sight, the KNOWLEDGE is what matters.'

"Hollond was embarking on a Socratic dialogue in which I could see little point. I told him so, and he laughed. "'I am not sure that I am very clear myself. But yes—there IS a point. Supposing you knew-not by sight or by instinct, but by sheer intellectual knowledge, as I know the truth of a mathematical proposition—that what we call empty space was full, crammed. Not with lumps of what we call matter like hills and houses, but with things as real—as real to the mind. Would you still feel crowded?'

"'No,' I said, 'I don't think so. It is only what we call matter that signifies. It would be just as well not to feel crowded by the other thing, for there would be no escape from it. But what are you getting at? Do you mean atoms or electric currents or what?'

"He said he wasn't thinking about that sort of thing, and began to talk of another subject.

"Next night, when we were pigging it at the Geant cabane, he started again on the same tack. He asked me how I accounted for the fact that animals could find their way back over great tracts of unknown country. I said I supposed it was the homing instinct.

"'Rubbish, man,' he said. 'That's only another name for the puzzle, not an explanation. There must be some reason for it. They must KNOW something that we cannot understand. Tie a cat in a bag and take it fifty miles by train and it will make its way home. That cat has some clue that we haven't.'

"I was tired and sleepy, and told him that I did not care a rush about the psychology of cats. But he was not to be snubbed, and went on talking.

"'How if Space is really full of things we cannot see and as yet do not know? How if all animals and some savages have a cell in their brain or a nerve which responds to the invisible world? How if all Space be full of these landmarks, not material in our sense, but quite real? A dog barks at nothing, a wild beast makes an aimless circuit. Why? Perhaps because Space is made up of corridors and alleys, ways to travel and things to shun? For all we know, to a greater intelligence than ours the top of Mont Blanc may be as crowded as Piccadilly Circus.'

"But at that point I fell asleep and left Hollond to repeat his questions to a guide who knew no English and a snoring porter.

"Six months later, one foggy January afternoon, Hollond rang me up at the Temple and proposed to come to see me that night after dinner. I thought he wanted to talk Alpine shop, but he turned up in Duke Street about nine with a kit-bag full of papers. He was an odd fellow to look at—a yellowish face with the skin stretched tight on the cheek-bones, clean-shaven, a sharp chin which he kept poking forward, and deep-set, greyish eyes. He was a hard fellow, too, always in pretty good condition, which was remarkable considering how he slaved for nine months out of the twelve. He had a quiet, slow-spoken manner, but that night I saw that he was considerably excited.

"He said that he had come to me because we were old friends. He proposed to tell me a tremendous secret. 'I must get another mind to work on it or I'll go crazy. I don't want a scientist. I want a plain man.'

"Then he fixed me with a look like a tragic actor's. 'Do you remember that talk we had in August at Chamonix—about Space? I daresay you thought I was playing the fool. So I was in a sense, but I was feeling my way towards something which has been in my mind for ten years. Now I have got it, and you must hear about it. You may take my word that it's a pretty startling discovery.'

"I lit a pipe and told him to go ahead, warning him that I knew about as much science as the dustman.

"I am bound to say that it took me a long time to understand what he meant. He began by saying that everybody thought of Space as an 'empty homogeneous medium.' 'Never mind at present what the ultimate constituents of that medium are. We take it as a finished product, and we think of it as mere extension, something without any quality at all. That is the view of civilised man. You will find all the philosophers taking it for granted. Yes, but every living thing does not take that view. An animal, for instance. It feels a kind of quality in Space. It can find its way over new country, because it perceives certain landmarks, not necessarily material, but perceptible, or if you like intelligible. Take an Australian savage. He has the same power, and, I believe, for the same reason. He is conscious of intelligible landmarks.'

"'You mean what people call a sense of direction,' I put in.

"'Yes, but what in Heaven's name is a sense of direction? The phrase explains nothing. However incoherent the mind of the animal or the savage may be, it is there somewhere, working on some data. I've been all through the psychological and anthropological side of the business, and after you eliminate the clues from sight and hearing and smell and half-conscious memory there remains a solid lump of the inexplicable.'

"Hollond's eye had kindled, and he sat doubled up in his chair, dominating me with a finger.

"'Here, then is a power which man is civilising himself out of. Call it anything you like, but you must admit that it is a power. Don't you see that it is a perception of another kind of reality that we are leaving behind us? ', Well, you know the way nature works. The wheel comes full circle, and what we think we have lost we regain in a higher form. So for a long time I have been wondering whether the civilised mind could not recreate for itself this lost gift, the gift of seeing the quality of Space. I mean that I wondered whether the scientific modern brain could not get to the stage of realising that Space is not an empty homogeneous medium, but full of intricate differences, intelligible and real, though not with our common reality.'

"I found all this very puzzling and he had to repeat it several times before I got a glimpse of what he was talking about.

"'I've wondered for a long time he went on 'but now quite suddenly, I have begun to know.' He stopped and asked me abruptly if I knew much about mathematics.

"'It's a pity,' he said,'but the main point is not technical, though I wish you could appreciate the beauty of some of my proofs. Then he began to tell me about his last six months' work. I should have mentioned that he was a brilliant physicist besides other things. All Hollond's tastes were on the borderlands of sciences, where mathematics fades into metaphysics and physics merges in the abstrusest kind of mathematics. Well, it seems he had been working for years at the ultimate problem of matter, and especially of that rarefied matter we call aether or space. I forget what his view was-atoms or molecules or electric waves. If he ever told me I have forgotten, but I'm not certain that I ever knew. However, the point was that these ultimate constituents were dynamic and mobile, not a mere passive medium but a medium in constant movement and change. He claimed to have discovered—by ordinary inductive experiment—that the constituents of aether possessed certain functions, and moved in certain figures obedient to certain mathematical laws. Space, I gathered, was perpetually 'forming fours' in some fancy way.

"Here he left his physics and became the mathematician. Among his mathematical discoveries had been certain curves or figures or something whose behaviour involved a new dimension. I gathered that this wasn't the ordinary Fourth Dimension that people talk of, but that fourth-dimensional inwardness or involution was part of it. The explanation lay in the pile of manuscripts he left with me, but though I tried honestly I couldn't get the hang of it. My mathematics stopped with desperate finality just as he got into his subject.

"His point was that the constituents of Space moved according to these new mathematical figures of his. They were always changing, but the principles of their change were as fixed as the law of gravitation. Therefore, if you once grasped these principles you knew the contents of the void. What do you make of that?"

I said that it seemed to me a reasonable enough argument, but that it got one very little way forward. "A man," I said, "might know the contents of Space and the laws of their arrangement and yet be unable to see anything more than his fellows. It is a purely academic knowledge. His mind knows it as the result of many deductions, but his senses perceive nothing."

Leithen laughed. "Just what I said to Hollond. He asked the opinion of my legal mind. I said I could not pronounce on his argument but that I could point out that he had established no trait d'union between the intellect which understood and the senses which perceived. It was like a blind man with immense knowledge but no eyes, and therefore no peg to hang his knowledge on and make it useful. He had not explained his savage or his cat. 'Hang it, man,' I said, 'before you can appreciate the existence of your Spacial forms you have to go through elaborate experiments and deductions. You can't be doing that every minute. Therefore you don't get any nearer to the USE of the sense you say that man once possessed, though you can explain it a bit.'"

"What did he say?" I asked.

"The funny thing was that he never seemed to see my difficulty. When I kept bringing him back to it he shied off with a new wild theory of perception. He argued that the mind can live in a world of realities without any sensuous stimulus to connect them with the world of our ordinary life. Of course that wasn't my point. I supposed that this world of Space was real enough to him, but I wanted to know how he got there. He never answered me. He was the typical Cambridge man, you know—dogmatic about uncertainties, but curiously diffident about the obvious. He laboured to get me to understand the notion of his mathematical forms, which I was quite willing to take on trust from him. Some queer things he said, too. He took our feeling about Left and Right as an example of our instinct for the quality of Space. But when I objected that Left and Right varied with each object, and only existed in connection with some definite material thing, he said that that was exactly what he meant. It was an example of the mobility of the Spacial forms. Do you see any sense in that?"

I shook my head. It seemed to me pure craziness.

"And then he tried to show me what he called the 'involution of Space,' by taking two points on a piece of paper. The points were a foot away when the paper was flat, they coincided when it was doubled up. He said that there were no gaps between the figures, for the medium was continuous, and he took as an illustration the loops on a cord. You are to think of a cord always looping and unlooping itself according to certain mathematical laws. Oh, I tell you, I gave up trying to follow him. And he was so desperately in earnest all the time. By his account Space was a sort of mathematical pandemonium."

Leithen stopped to refill his pipe, and I mused upon the ironic fate which had compelled a mathematical genius to make his sole confidant of a philistine lawyer, and induced that lawyer to repeat it confusedly to an ignoramus at twilight on a Scotch hill. As told by Leithen it was a very halting tale.

"But there was one thing I could see very clearly," Leithen went on, "and that was Hollond's own case. This crowded world of Space was perfectly real to him. How he had got to it I do not know. Perhaps his mind, dwelling constantly on the problem, had unsealed some atrophied cell and restored the old instinct. Anyhow, he was living his daily life with a foot in each world.

"He often came to see me, and after the first hectic discussions he didn't talk much. There was no noticeable change in him—a little more abstracted perhaps. He would walk in the street or come into a room with a quick look round him, and sometimes for no earthly reason he would swerve. Did you ever watch a cat crossing a room? It sidles along by the furniture and walks over an open space of carpet as if it were picking its way among obstacles. Well, Hollond behaved like that, but he had always been counted a little odd, and nobody noticed it but me.

"I knew better than to chaff him, and had stopped argument, so there wasn't much to be said. But sometimes he would give me news about his experiences. The whole thing was perfectly clear and scientific and above board, and nothing creepy about it. You know how I hate the washy supernatural stuff they give us nowadays. Hollond was well and fit, with an appetite like a hunter. But as he talked, sometimes—well, you know I haven't much in the way of nerves or imagination—but I used to get a little eerie. Used to feel the solid earth dissolving round me. It was the opposite of vertigo, if you understand me—a sense of airy realities crowding in on you-crowding the mind, that is, not the body.

"I gathered from Hollond that he was always conscious of corridors and halls and alleys in Space, shifting, but shifting according to inexorable laws. I never could get quite clear as to what this consciousness was like. When I asked he used to look puzzled and worried and helpless. I made out from him that one landmark involved a sequence, and once given a bearing from an object you could keep the direction without a mistake. He told me he could easily, if he wanted, go in a dirigible from the top of Mont Blanc to the top of Snowdon in the thickest fog and without a compass, if he were given the proper angle to start from. I confess I didn't follow that myself. Material objects had nothing to do with the Spacial forms, for a table or a bed in our world might be placed across a corridor of Space. The forms played their game independent of our kind of reality. But the worst of it was, that if you kept your mind too much in one world you were apt to forget about the other and Hollond was always barking his shins on stones and chairs and things.

"He told me all this quite simply and frankly. Remember his mind and no other part of him lived in his new world. He said it gave him an odd sense of detachment to sit in a room among people, and to know that nothing there but himself had any relation at all to the infinite strange world of Space that flowed around them. He would listen, he said, to a great man talking, with one eye on the cat on the rug, thinking to himself how much more the cat knew than the man."

"How long was it before he went mad?" I asked.

It was a foolish question, and made Leithen cross. "He never went mad in your sense. My dear fellow, you're very much wrong if you think there was anything pathological about him—then. The man was brilliantly sane. His mind was as keen is a keen sword. I couldn't understand him, but I could judge of his sanity right enough."

I asked if it made him happy or miserable.

"At first I think it made him uncomfortable. He was restless because he knew too much and too little. The unknown pressed in on his mind as bad air weighs on the lungs. Then it lightened and he accepted the new world in the same sober practical way that he took other things. I think that the free exercise of his mind in a pure medium gave him a feeling of extraordinary power and ease. His eyes used to sparkle when he talked. And another odd thing he told me. He was a keen rockclimber, but, curiously enough, he had never a very good head. Dizzy heights always worried him, though he managed to keep hold on himself. But now all that had gone. The sense of the fulness of Space made him as happy—happier I believe—with his legs dangling into eternity, as sitting before his own study fire.

"I remember saying that it was all rather like the mediaeval wizards who made their spells by means of numbers and figures.

"He caught me up at once. 'Not numbers,' he said. "Number has no place in Nature. It is an invention of the human mind to atone for a bad memory. But figures are a different matter. All the mysteries of the world are in them, and the old magicians knew that at least, if they knew no more.'

"He had only one grievance. He complained that it was terribly lonely. 'It is the Desolation,' he would quote, 'spoken of by Daniel the prophet.' He would spend hours travelling those eerie shifting corridors of Space with no hint of another human soul. How could there be? It was a world of pure reason, where human personality had no place. What puzzled me was why he should feel the absence of this. One wouldn't you know, in an intricate problem of geometry or a game of chess. I asked him, but he didn't understand the question. I puzzled over it a good deal, for it seemed to me that if Hollond felt lonely, there must be more in this world of his than we imagined. I began to wonder if there was any truth in fads like psychical research. Also, I was not so sure that he was as normal as I had thought: it looked as if his nerves might be going bad.

"Oddly enough, Hollond was getting on the same track himself. He had discovered, so he said, that in sleep everybody now and then lived in this new world of his. You know how one dreams of triangular railway platforms with trains running simultaneously down all three sides and not colliding. Well, this sort of cantrip was 'common form,' as we say at the Bar, in Hollond's Space, and he was very curious about the why and wherefore of Sleep. He began to haunt psychological laboratories, where they experiment with the charwoman and the odd man, and he used to go up to Cambridge for seances. It was a foreign atmosphere to him, and I don't think he was very happy in it. He found so many charlatans that he used to get angry, and declare he would be better employed at Mother's Meetings!"

From far up the Glen came the sound of the pony's hoofs. The stag had been loaded up and the gillies were returning. Leithen looked at his watch. "We'd better wait and see the beast," he said.

"... Well, nothing happened for more than a year. Then one evening in May he burst into my rooms in high excitement. You understand quite clearly that there was no suspicion of horror or fright or anything unpleasant about this world he had discovered. It was simply a series of interesting and difficult problems. All this time Hollond had been rather extra well and cheery. But when he came in I thought I noticed a different look in his eyes, something puzzled and diffident and apprehensive.

"'There's a queer performance going on in the other world,' he said. 'It's unbelievable. I never dreamed of such a thing. I—I don't quite know how to put it, and I don't know how to explain it, but—but I am becoming aware that there are other beings—other minds—moving in Space besides mine.'

"I suppose I ought to have realised then that things were beginning to go wrong. But it was very difficult, he was so rational and anxious to make it all clear. I asked him how he knew. 'There could, of course, on his own showing be no CHANGE in that world, for the forms of Space moved and existed under inexorable laws. He said he found his own mind failing him at points. There would come over him a sense of fear—intellectual fear—and weakness, a sense of something else, quite alien to Space, thwarting him. Of course he could only describe his impressions very lamely, for they were purely of the mind, and he had no material peg to hang them on, so that I could realise them. But the gist of it was that he had been gradually becoming conscious of what he called 'Presences' in his world. They had no effect on Space—did not leave footprints in its corridors, for instance—but they affected his mind.

There was some mysterious contact established between him and them. I asked him if the affection was unpleasant and he said 'No, not exactly.' But I could see a hint of fear in his eyes.

"Think of it. Try to realise what intellectual fear is. I can't, but it is conceivable. To you and me fear implies pain to ourselves or some other, and such pain is always in the last resort pain of the flesh. Consider it carefully and you will see that it is so. But imagine fear so sublimated and transmuted as to be the tension of pure spirit. I can't realise it, but I think it possible. I don't pretend to understand how Hollond got to know about these Presences. But there was no doubt about the fact. He was positive, and he wasn't in the least mad—not in our sense. In that very month he published his book on Number, and gave a German professor who attacked it a most tremendous public trouncing.

"I know what you are going to say,—that the fancy was a weakening of the mind from within. I admit I should have thought of that but he looked so confoundedly sane and able that it seemed ridiculous. He kept asking me my opinion, as a lawyer, on the facts he offered. It was the oddest case ever put before me, but I did my best for him. I dropped all my own views of sense and nonsense. I told him that, taking all that he had told me as fact, the Prescences might be either ordinary minds traversing Space in sleep; or minds such as his which had independently captured the sense of Space's quality; or, finally, the spirits of just men made perfect, behaving as psychical researchers think they do. It was a ridiculous task to set a prosaic man, and I wasn't quite serious. But Holland was serious enough.

"He admitted that all three explanations were conceivable, but he was very doubtful about the first. The projection of the spirit into Space during sleep, he thought, was a faint and feeble thing, and these were powerful Presences. With the second and the third he was rather impressed. I suppose I should have seen what was happening and tried to stop it; at least, looking back that seems to have been my duty. But it was difficult to think that anything was wrong with Hollond; indeed the odd thing is that all this time the idea of madness never entered my head. I rather backed him up. Somehow the thing took my fancy, though I thought it moonshine at the bottom of my heart. I enlarged on the pioneering before him. 'Think,' I told him, 'what may be waiting for you. You may discover the meaning of Spirit. You may open up a new world, as rich as the old one, but imperishable. You may prove to mankind their immortality and deliver them for ever from the fear of death. Why, man, you are picking at the lock of all the world's mysteries.'

"But Hollond did not cheer up. He seemed strangely languid and dispirited. 'That is all true enough,' he said,'if you are right, if your alternatives are exhaustive. But suppose they are something else, something .... What that 'something' might be he had apparently no idea, and very soon he went away.

"He said another thing before he left. He asked me if I ever read poetry, and I said, not often. Nor did he: but he had picked up a little book somewhere and found a man who knew about the Presences. I think his name was Traherne, one of the seventeenth-century fellows. He quoted a verse which stuck to my fly-paper memory. It ran something like

'Within the region of the air,
Compassed about with Heavens fair,
Great tracts of lands there may be found,
Where many numerous hosts,
In those far distant coasts,
For other great and glorious ends
Inhabit, my yet unknown friends.'

Hollond was positive he did not mean angels or anything of the sort. I told him that Traherne evidently took a cheerful view of them. He admitted that, but added: 'He had religion, you see. He believed that everything was for the best. I am not a man of faith, and can only take comfort from what I understand. I'm in the dark, I tell you...'

"Next week I was busy with the Chilian Arbitration case, and saw nobody for a couple of months. Then one evening I ran against Hollond on the Embankment, and thought him looking horribly ill. He walked back with me to my rooms, and hardly uttered one word all the way. I gave him a stiff whisky-and-soda, which he gulped down absent-mindedly. There was that strained, hunted look in his eyes that you see in a frightened animal's. He was always lean, but now he had fallen away to skin and bone.

"'I can't stay long,' he told me, 'for I'm off to the Alps to-morrow and I have a lot to do.' Before then he used to plunge readily into his story, but now he seemed shy about beginning. Indeed I had to ask him a question.

"'Things are difficult,' he said hesitatingly, and rather distressing. Do you know, Leithen, I think you were wrong about—about what I spoke to you of. You said there must be one of three explanations. I am beginning to think that there is a fourth.

"He stopped for a second or two, then suddenly leaned forward and gripped my knee so fiercely that I cried out. 'That world is the Desolation,' he said in a choking voice, 'and perhaps I am getting near the Abomination of the Desolation that the old prophet spoke of. I tell you, man, I am on the edge of a terror, a terror,' he almost screamed, 'that no mortal can think of and live.'

You can imagine that I was considerably startled. It was lightning out of a clear sky. How the devil could one associate horror with mathematics? I don't see it yet... At any rate, I—You may be sure I cursed my folly for ever pretending to take him seriously. The only way would have been to have laughed him out of it at the start. And yet I couldn't, you know—it was too real and reasonable. Anyhow, I tried a firm tone now, and told him the whole thing was arrant raving bosh. I bade him be a man and pull himself together. I made him dine with me, and took him home, and got him into a better state of mind before he went to bed. Next morning I saw him off at Charing Cross, very haggard still, but better. He promised to write to me pretty often....

The pony, with a great eleven-pointer lurching athwart its back, was abreast of us, and from the autumn mist came the sound of soft Highland voices. Leithen and I got up to go, when we heard that the rifle had made direct for the Lodge by a short cut past the Sanctuary. In the wake of the gillies we descended the Correi road into a glen all swimming with dim purple shadows. The pony minced and boggled; the stag's antlers stood out sharp on the rise against a patch of sky, looking like a skeleton tree. Then we dropped into a covert of birches and emerged on the white glen highway.

Leithen's story had bored and puzzled me at the start, but now it had somehow gripped my fancy. Space a domain of endless corridors and Presences moving in them! The world was not quite the same as an hour ago. It was the hour, as the French say, "between dog and wolf," when the mind is disposed to marvels. I thought of my stalking on the morrow, and was miserably conscious that I would miss my stag. Those airy forms would get in the way. Confound Leithen and his yarns!

"I want to hear the end of your story," I told him, as the lights of the Lodge showed half a mile distant.

"The end was a tragedy," he said slowly. "I don't much care to talk about it. But how was I to know? I couldn't see the nerve going. You see I couldn't believe it was all nonsense. If I could I might have seen. But I still think there was something in it—up to a point. Oh, I agree he went mad in the end. It is the only explanation. Something must have snapped in that fine brain, and he saw the little bit more which we call madness. Thank God, you and I are prosaic fellows...

"I was going out to Chamonix myself a week later. But before I started I got a post-card from Hollond, the only word from him. He had printed my name and address, and on the other side had scribbled six words—'I know at last—God's mercy.—H.G.H' The handwriting was like a sick man of ninety. I knew that things must be pretty bad with my friend.

"I got to Chamonix in time for his funeral. An ordinary climbing accident —you probably read about it in the papers. The Press talked about the toll which the Alps took from intellectuals—the usual rot. There was an inquiry, but the facts were quite simple. The body was only recognised by the clothes. He had fallen several thousand feet.

"It seems that he had climbed for a few days with one of the Kronigs and Dupont, and they had done some hair-raising things on the Aiguilles. Dupont told me that they had found a new route up the Montanvert side of the Charmoz. He said that Hollond climbed like a 'diable fou' and if you know Dupont's standard of madness you will see that the pace must have been pretty hot. 'But monsieur was sick,' he added; 'his eyes were not good. And I and Franz, we were grieved for him and a little afraid. We were glad when he left us.'

"He dismissed the guides two days before his death. The next day he spent in the hotel, getting his affairs straight. He left everything in perfect order, but not a line to a soul, not even to his sister. The following day he set out alone about three in the morning for the Grepon. He took the road up the Nantillons glacier to the Col, and then he must have climbed the Mummery crack by himself. After that he left the ordinary route and tried a new traverse across the Mer de Glace face. Somewhere near the top he fell, and next day a party going to the Dent du Requin found him on the rocks thousands of feet below.

"He had slipped in attempting the most foolhardy course on earth, and there was a lot of talk about the dangers of guideless climbing. But I guessed the truth, and I am sure Dupont knew, though he held his tongue...."

We were now on the gravel of the drive, and I was feeling better. The thought of dinner warmed my heart and drove out the eeriness of the twilight glen. The hour between dog and wolf was passing. After all, there was a gross and jolly earth at hand for wise men who had a mind to comfort.

Leithen, I saw, did not share my mood. He looked glum and puzzled, as if his tale had aroused grim memories. He finished it at the Lodge door.

"... For, of course, he had gone out that day to die. He had seen the something more, the little bit too much, which plucks a man from his moorings. He had gone so far into the land of pure spirit that he must needs go further and shed the fleshly envelope that cumbered him. God send that he found rest! I believe that he chose the steepest cliff in the Alps for a purpose. He wanted to be unrecognisable. He was a brave man and a good citizen. I think he hoped that those who found him might not see the look in his eyes."

Space was published in *The Moon Endureth—Tales and Fancies,* published in 1912. This version of the story was taken from Project Gutenberg.

Reviews

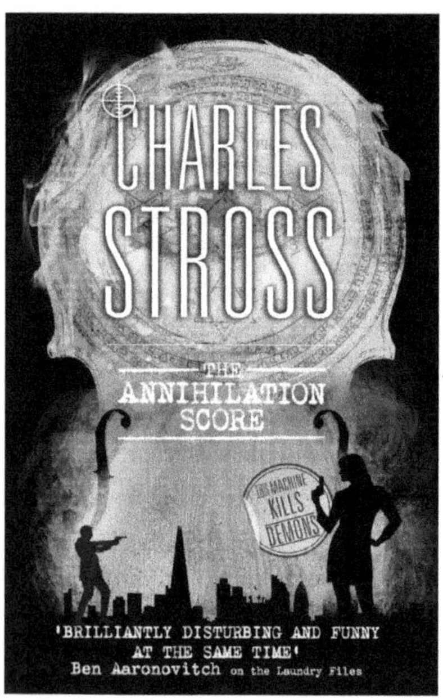

The Annihilation Score
Charles Stross
Orbit
£16.99, hardback, 416pp.
published 2nd July 2014

Review: Noel Chidwick

Bob Howard, the newly anointed Eater of Souls, leaves stage right to pursue bears. Meanwhile, his wife Mo, steps up to the footlights. Under her chin she tucks her possessed killer violin made of human bone, and is ready to take on the latest problem to hit humanity—an exponential increase of the population developing super powers. How will Mo and the Laundry save us?

If what I've written so far makes little sense, then do yourself a massive favour and read Charles Stross' series the *Laundry Files*. You'll be thoroughly entertained as Bob takes on the demons released on the world using only his wits and his occult skills nurtured as IT support for an off-line anti-supernatural government body.

Back here, at book 7, we at last get to hear Mo's story, working with her to save humanity and explore her anxieties. This is also Stross balancing the gender books:

> "The invisible man is a Wellsian supervillain, but the invisible women are all around us, anxious and unseen."

How do you find out what the ultimate Supervillain, Dr Freudstein, is up to? How do you stop him? The Laundry decides to set Mo—Dr Dominique O'Brien—the task of heading up a small department with a management team with their own variations of superpowers. This team includes Mhari the vampire who was once Bob's girlfriend, Ramone, transitioning to a mermaid who once shared Bob's mind, and Officer Friendly, the superhero cop whose stone jaw juts out further than the jetty at Lyme Regis. What could go wrong?

They gather field workers with superpowers, including Lollipop Bill, Captain Mahvelous and Busy Bee. After deciding half-heartedly what they should wear—no corsets nor fishnet stockings and eschewing the capes—off they go.

But Mo has plenty of her own inner demons to contend with, including her self-doubts, worrying about her relationship with her husband, and the responsibility of setting up this team. And to complicate things further Lecter, her demon killing violin, seeps into her dreams and her mind, threatening to take control.

Annihilation Score is trademark Stross, mingling the mundane intricacies of modern office life with the ever present fear of damnation and the end of the world. The book would make for an entertaining a "management team for dummies" instruction manual, and perhaps some imaginative management lecturers will offer this as a set text. Stross delights in playing with the absurdities of life acted out in millions of workplaces around the planet: the world will not end with a bang, but an e-mail.

The climax of the story is suitably grandiose to satisfy all fans of the Laundry files, where Stross' tight plotting and fast-pace action knit together while we cheer and laugh from the safety of behind the sofa.

Annihilation Score is a thrilling journey on our way towards CASE NIGHTMARE GREEN, and now we look forward to following up on Bob *Eater of Souls* Howard's exploits in the next book.

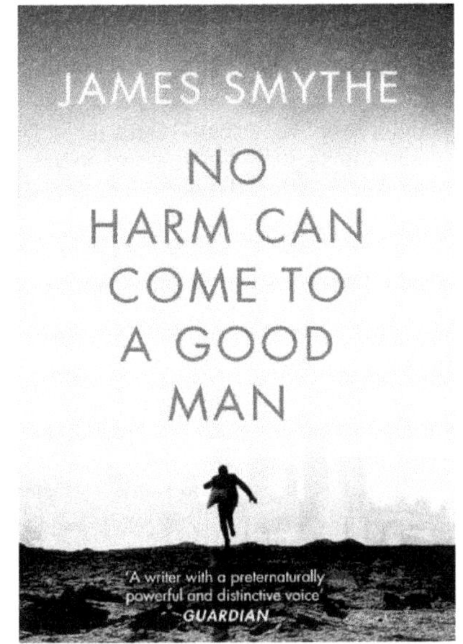

No Harm Can Come to a Good Man
James Smyth
The Borough Press,
£7.99, paperback, 374 pp.
Review: Duncan Lunan

Well, a title like that should warn you. Laurence Walker is in line for the Democratic nomination to run for President of the United States. He is something of a war hero, having been captured in combat and withstood torture under which others have cracked. He is married with a son and two daughters, appears to have no skeletons in the cupboard, and his campaign is likely to attract major backers.

Everything looks good except that his principal opponent Homme (Everyman?) has beaten him in the race to be first with a computer prediction of success. This is a near-future world in which that counts for a great deal, because most major decisions are taken with reference to a predictive computer system called ClearVista, whose latest market version will even show you a snapshot video of a moment from your future life. Homme's shows him on a Presidential visit to armed forces in the field; Walker's, when produced, gives him zero chance of nomination or election, and shows him covering his family with a gun. Protests that ClearVista doesn't predict what *will* happen are of no avail: the Party, the media and the public all respond on the basis that if it *could* happen, that's enough for them. What follows has the inevitably of *Macbeth*, with the difference that Walker and his political advisor are trying to prevent the prophecy from being believed, much less coming true, rather than trying to bring about what it predicts.

My life as a reviewer is filled with strange coincidences, and this book has come my way just as my critical notes on the classic *Jeff Hawke* and *Lance McLane* comic strips, being published with reprints of the strips by the Jeff Hawke Club, have reached the point where their creator Sydney Jordan became increasingly preoccupied with destiny and foreordination. One of the major issues of philosophy is how (if at all) determinism and causality can be reconciled with free will, and as it happens, I found myself reading *No Harm Can Come to a Good Man* in parallel with *The Emperor's New Mind* by Roger Penrose. One of the major themes of that book is how that philosophical debate relates to the practicality of artificial intelligence, and the provocative conclusion was that free will (a) is demonstrable, (b) cannot be simulated by algorithmic processes, so ruling out artifical intelligence in that form, now and for all time. The heavy emphasis in *No Harm Can Come...* upon the algorithmic nature of ClearVista's predictions might suggest that Smythe has taken his inspiration from Penrose's book, and has set out to show us just how far wrong things could go, following Penrose's logic to its conclusions, should people put their trust in such predictions nevertheless.

This is no abstract philosophical text, though – it follows Walker's decline and fall in entirely human terms. In that respect it has a lot in common with Susan Barker's *Incarnations*, which I reviewed last year for *Concatenation*: both show a flawed but basically decent man being overwhelmed by predictions about his future, from an apparently all-knowing source, against which he struggles in vain. The title has the same force as that moment in a disaster movie, when someone who should know better assures the other characters that absolutely nothing can go wrong.

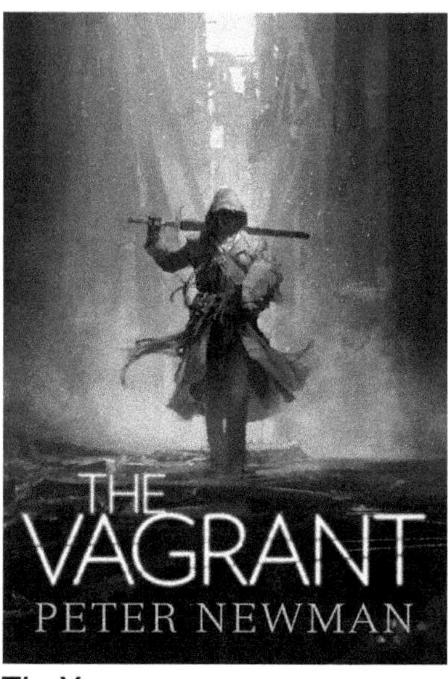

The Vagrant
Peter Newman
Harper Voyager
£14.99, hardback, 400pp.
Review: Ian Hunter

He is "The Vagrant", that "is his name. He has no other" proclaims the cover, below a cover illustration – by whom? I don't know as this is clearly a very advance proof copy, so there is no mention of the illustrator and there are blanks for the author's dedication and acknowledgements, although the cover is slightly misleading as we are given a hooded figure (so hooded that his face is in shadow),who wears a tattered coat, with one hand balancing a sword across his shoulders, while his other hand holds a bundle of baby close to his chest, and all this beneath a looming cityscape, crowding in on him from both sides. I say, misleading because The Vagrant we read beyond this cover would never be so brazen to reveal the fabled sword that he carries or the baby tucked within the confines of his coat. Both are precious to him. The sword is a lost treasure, bearing great power that many covet, because of its worth or because they want to see it – and the forces of darkness christen the weapon "The Malice" – destroyed. The baby is also coveted, but it's probably better not to dwell on why and what for in a world where body parts of the living and dead are sought after. As for the name "Vagrant"? Given that our hero cannot utter a word, and has to communicate by facial expressions and gestures, I'd be hard pressed to remember an instance when someone else, other than Newman, actually refers to our wandering hero as "The Vagrant", although he does gather a few other names along the way.

Eight years ago, ten thousand Seraph Knights fought in the Battle of the Red Wave, fighting on the side of the Empire of the Winged Eye, fighting alongside Gamma, one of the fabled, all-mighty, Seven, but the Seven have been complacent, too remote from human affairs in their ivory towers in the Shining City. It has taken them over a year to deliberate what to do when the first demonic hordes started rising from the Breach, and when they finally decide to fight, those that have risen from the Breach have a foothold in this world and are waiting for them. Incredibly, Gamma falls, along with eight thousand knights, and soon the two thousand that remain are reduced to only a handful, and the world around the Breach starts to change, become malignant, and the demonic entity known as the Usurper is created and eight years later, travelling across this devastated world walks a stranger, a man with a mission, bearing two secrets - gamma's sword and a baby, and he has to get them both to the Shining City.

I'm reminded of that line out of *Amadeus* when the King complains to Mozart that his music has "too many notes", and if you've ever listened to the jazz compositions or classical music that Frank Zappa wrote, you'll know what I mean as they are just too busy. There is a heck of a lot going on in Newman's debut novel as we journey with the Vagrant and various "hangers on" and encounter a whole host of exotic characters and equally exotic, or decaying locations. The invention here is probably on a par with the "Arabat" novels of Clive Barker, the series of Fourth World DC comics of the late Jack Kirby, and more recently "The Relic Guild" by Edward Cox. Rather like Cox's novel the story is told in a linear fashion, punctuated by a series of past events, that become more and more recent, thus we learn of the Breach being breached and the fall of Gamma, right up until a year ago, and these glimpses into the past reveal the story of the Vagrant, why he carries Gamma's sword and whom the baby belongs to. Given that this is an uncorrected proof copy, some of these chapters set in the past did slip into the present when I think they should have been a brand new chapter, no doubt something that will be corrected for the final edition.

"The Vagrant" isn't really my cup of tea, and I had problems with all the situations and scenarios and the denseness of the description in places and a lack of lead character viewpoint, in a writing style that reminded me of William Gibson and Gene Wolfe because of its tendency to distance things slightly through a present tense, observational delivery. Credibility was also stretched in for too many places where the plot could be termed as "and with one mighty leap the Vagrant was free". Yet, despite these misgivings, I did devour whole chunks of the novel at one sitting, and I did even start to care about the minor characters, even the goat that gets dragged along behind them to provide milk for the infant. One character in particular showed interesting character development and could have spawned a few interesting plot lines, but no, Newman ruthlessly cut them down, or rather the Vagrant did, albeit reluctantly. He is the archetypal hero, the stranger, on a quest, on a mission. The man with almost no name that changes everything. He does not speak nor do we get into his head, rather we see how he reacts and interacts with others and the effect he has on the lives of those he encounters, a flickering light of hope in a land of darkness. I look forward to seeing how that effect continues in the sequel called "The Malice" due out next year.

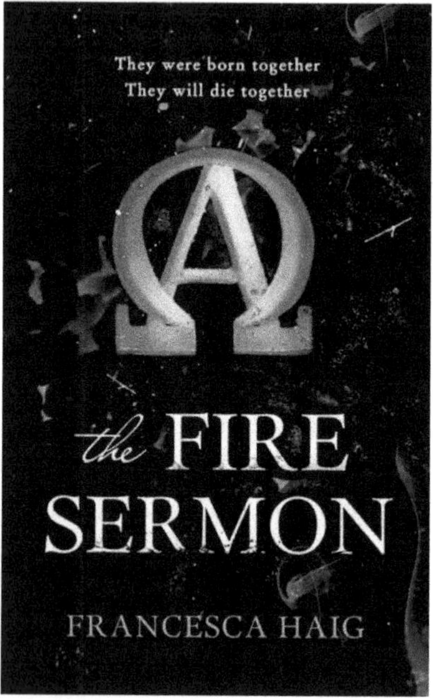

The Fire Sermon
Francesca Haig
Harper Collins
£12.99, hardback, 419pp
Review: Noel Chidwick

***The Fire Sermon* is a novel that hits** the ground galloping, scooping up Cass onto the back of a horse to be thrown into a dungeon lit only by the buzzing glow of a single lightbulb. Chapter one is a masterclass for fledgling writers in how to grab your readers by the eyeballs and hurl them into your story.

Some 400 years after the 'Blast' mankind is back to pre-industrial existence, but with a twist. Births are always boy-girl twins where one—the Alpha—is perfect, but the other—the Omega—is deformed in some way. The deformation is usually visible and the Omega twin sent away. But sometimes the deformation is not obvious and the twins are brought up together until the Omega becomes apparent. Cass—short for Cassandra, unnecessarily—the Omega twin to Zach hides her 'deformation' for years until as teenagers she finally has to reveal that she is a seer, sensing events to come. She dreams of the Blast too:

"There were no written tales... what was the point...when it was etched on every surface? It was still visible in every tumbled cliff, scorched plain and every ash-clogged river. Every face. It had become the only story the earth could tell, so who else would record it?"

Yes, the first thought that sprang to my mind is John Wyndham's The Chrysalids. Set in a similar post-nuclear apocalypse where the deformed infants are similarly scorned, and the protagonist whose 'deformity' is similarly of the mind, in this case David being a telepath. But Francesca Haig sets us old-timers' minds at rest when she cheekily names her main town where Cass is incarcerated as Wyndham. Thereafter I relaxed into the tale to see where we are taken.

The Fire Sermon relies on the new cast-iron law of nature of linked twins (when one dies, so does the other) and the story rattles along as we understand Cass was imprisoned by her twin who by now is a High Heid Yin on the Council, who is protecting his sister in the cell and thereby protecting himself.

Soon Cass is on the run with her new friend Kip as they try to find their way to a safe colony for Omegas and the story becomes a strong chase around this neatly described future of mankind knocked back to an agricultural lifestyle. We sympathise with Cass as she struggles internally to understand her world, how to restore her relationship with her brother and also right the wrongs of the persecution of the Omegas. Although a contrivance, the linking of severe pain and deaths of twins sets up an agonising balance, asking us to consider that when we harm others we also risk injuring ourselves. I rattled through the book, eager to turn the page. It's a mix of adventure and plot turns, with ample space to explore themes of oppression and reconciliation.

Wyndham fans may well each raise an eyebrow, but they can lower them again: The Fire Sermon is a thoroughly good read. It is craftfully written and reaches a satisfying conclusion, but with enough loose ends to guarantee the story continues. I look forward to the sequel to be published in the New Year.

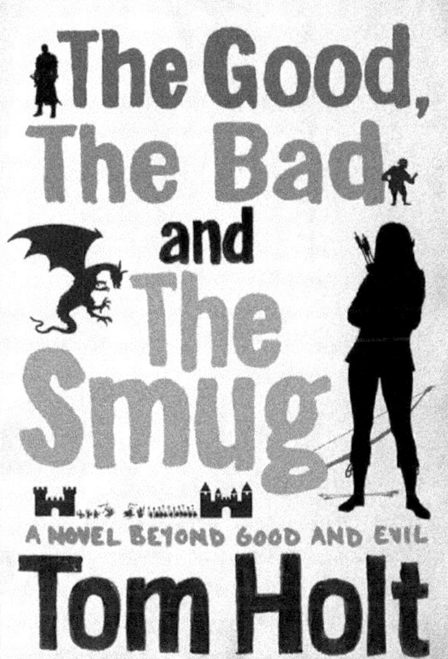

The Good, The Bad and The Smug
Tom Holt
Orbit
£8.99, paperback, 368pp
published 30th July 2015
Review: Jacob Edwards

What's in a name?

Book covers of old would sometimes describe Tom Holt's writing as *seriously funny*, and because the *funny* aspect was predominant there was a tendency to assume *seriously* was being used in the informal sense; to wit, *substantially*. But it would also be true (if somewhat more demanding on the rolling tongue) to call Holt *funnily serious*, and over the last umpteen years the tone of his books has been darkening slowly towards this inversion. The words *black comedy* have come by way of misappropriation elsewhere to indicate a non-comedic work, particularly a flop, trying to shift genres and pass itself off with imperial majesty, but in Holt's case the term might genuinely be applied. Earlier this year, he came out as the author behind award-winning pseudonymous fantasy writer K. J. Parker — not altogether surprising; the acknowledgments page at the back of Parker's novel *Sharps*, where she describes herself as overweight and middle-aged, was clearly a prelude to confession — and if his/her bodies of work are examined in parallel, a certain amount of cross-pollination is indeed discernible.

Tom Holt is both serious and funny, and it is this blend, this melding of authorial attributes, that gives his books their mouth-watering allure.

The Good, the Bad and the Smug is the fourth and most recent of Holt's forays into YouSpace (an operating system that affords its users access to the multiverse, using portals invoked by looking through the eye of a doughnut). Its tagline is *a novel beyond good and evil*, and though the paronomastic title renders unto this a certain levity, Holt's exploration takes us outside the box and in fact allows for some atypical, rather sobering perspectives on this not-quite-so-unambiguous tenet of human existence.

The book is still gently uproarious (fair dinkum droll, as we say in Australia), but whether due to subject matter or delivery, it's also just a tad less accessible than usual. One contributing factor must be that, with the exception of the South Cudworth and District Particle Physics Club (unforgettably hapless in trying to bake a doughnut), the protagonists are all non-human: there's Mordak, the nominally bad yet progressively enlightened king of the goblins; Efluviel, an elf driven by self-interest but made to detour along the road of *doing the right thing*; Archie, a goblin enduring human form; a rogue commodities broker (technically human, but...); and the Dark Lord himself, whose millennia of incorporeal floating have given rise finally to a new body with in-built, not-so-dark motivations.

To a fault these characters either exhibit or experience human foibles, their alien mind-sets giving *homo sapien* the chance to stand outside looking in; and perhaps at heart this is what makes the book ever so slightly uncomfortable a read: humanity is bad enough when it's happening *to* you; to step back and find it's just *happening*, and that you're an inseparable part of it, well, that's enough to make a person dash for the nearest bakery...

In a multiverse all things are possible, so anything we can imagine, no matter how absurd, must take place; and while the bad news is that it mostly seems to be taking place in our particular universe, the good news is that we have Tom Holt (quoz-finder by royal appointment, somewhere at least) to point it out to us: the film industry; gala awards nights; journalism and bureaucracy; prophesy; quest fantasy; interactive operating systems; grand scale economic policy; good and evil; the whole shebang. If it's going on and really, by any measure of common sense, shouldn't be, expect to read about it in a Tom Holt novel. (Or in more sombre tones, distilled down to the essence of human nature, something by K. J. Parker; and if you've read one but not the other, you have a lot to catch up on.)

The Good, the Bad and the Smug is Holt's first book since owning up to the Parker pen name — rarely has a pun waited so long to germinate — and to anybody who might fret as to his ongoing efficacy as a humourist, it should serve to assuage all worry.

Tom Holt remains his usual, vivid, parlously witty self. All told, in fact, he's now twice as accomplished as you probably thought.

Coming Up in Issue 2

We have some great stories prepared for you, again by some writers you will recognise, others who will be new to you. *SF Caledonia* will feature a story by Duncan Lunan - a pillar of Scottish Science Fiction. We will also be talking to Duncan about his life and writing.

We're opening up a whole new SF poetry section—*Multiverse*. This is edited by a newcomer to the team, Russell Jones. Russell is an Edinburgh based writer, poet and editor, and brings a whole bag of energy and talent to *Shoreline of Infinity*. He has something rather interesting lined up for us.

Issue 2 will be out in December 2015. From then on *Shoreline of Infinity* will be published quarterly.

Meet the Artists

Dave Alexander *(The Brat and the Burly Qs, Website banner)* was born and dragged up in Glasgow in the mid 20th century—in a time of steam trains, tramcars and black and white tv.

He was bitten by the science fiction bug (eyed monster?) at an early age, through the combined onslaught of comics, picture cards, SF films and television. He trained as a technical illustrator, inspired by the cutaway illustrations he had seen in *Eagle* comic. he painted covers for D.C. Thomson's *Starblazer* comics.

He turned to drawing and publishing his own comics—the adult humour titles 'Electric Soup' in 1989, and Northern Lightz in 1999.

Monica Burns *(Space)* a new graduate from the University of St Andrews and just starting out as a freelance illustrator. She enjoys reading Sci-Fi and Fantasy books—they never fail to inspire her art. She loves to tell stories and depict interesting scenarios through her drawings. **tinyurl.com/shorelinemonica**

Becca McCall, *(Three Stages of Atsushi, Cleanup on Deck Seven)* Born in Glasgow 1987, studied computer animation with digital art and the University of the West of Scotland, she's been painting and drawing as a hobby since she could hold a pencil. She loves to work with all sorts of mediums such as watercolours and inks, and to experiment different styles. She currently does various graphics for the Britannia Panopticon. **www.flickr.com/photos/beccamccall**

P. Emerson Williams *(Broken Glass)* is an artist, musician, actor and writer who works in a creative continuum that draws upon an interest in the arcane and esoteric. His passion is for embodying the mythic in visual media and melding visual art with narrative form. **pemersonwilliams.wordpress.com**

Bill Wright's work *(Front Cover)* is bold and provocative in its portrayal of science fiction hardware and astronomical art. Starting out using traditional media he was well represented on the Science Fiction convention scene for many years. Illustrations appear in *STEM* and *Perihelian* magazine on line and in print. He is also published by The Planetary Society and The National Space Society. **www.flickr.com/photos/billwrigt1**/

Alex Storer *(TimeMachineStory)* is an artist/illustrator and musician based in Sheffield, UK. A lifelong interest in science fiction came full circle in 2010 when Alex began producing his own artwork, taking influence from classic SF and the space art greats of the 1970s and 80s. In 2012, Alex was invited to be first honorary musician/ artist for the Initiative for Interstellar Studies. **www.thelightdream.net**

Sara Ljeskovac *(Approaching 43,000 Candles, Spiral Moon)* is a Swiss-born geek who lives in lovely Edinburgh. She has drawn for as long as she can remember and has always loved science fiction, space, and fantasy stories (Star Trek TOS & Twilight Zone being major influences). She is interested in book illustration and comics. **www.saraljart.com**

Stephen Pickering *(See You Later, Story Competition)* lives near Dumfries, Scotland. He is an Edwardian Gentleman by nature.

Mark Toner *(Symbiosis)* We like to give our Art Director a chance to show off his skills too. **www.spacepilot.scot**

Friends of Shoreline

Our infinite gratitude goes to these fine folk. They all subscribed to *Shoreline of Infinity* and we are proud to share their names with our readers. You are each and everyone of you welcome to pull up a log, warm your hands on our driftwood fire and listen to the marvellous tales told by our authors.

Thank you, Priti Barua
Thank you, Jill Ann Mcdonell Braybrook
Thank you, Collin Camepbell
Thank you, Molly Davis
Thank you, Turner Docherty
Thank you, Rich Dodgin
Thank you, Susan Duncan
Thank you, Lea Fletcher
Thank you, Sam Fleming
Thank you, Andrew Foster
Thank you, John Fulton
Thank you, Shivani Ganguly
Thank you, Daniel Haskovec
Thank you, Rusty Hodge
Thank you, Jules David Koperwas
Thank you, Laura La Gassa
Thank you, David LaMacchia
Thank you, Eolwaen Linden
Thank you, Alan MacGillivray
Thank you, Dennis Mahle
Thank you, Iain Maloney
Thank you, S.H. Mansouri
Thank you, Nick McDonell
Thank you, Nancee McDonell
Thank you, Roland McGrath
Thank you, Daniele Mills
Thank you, J. Hiroshi Morisaki
Thank you, Aneel Nazareth
Thank you, Susan Oke
Thank you, Patricia Pickering
Thank you, Rebecca & Andy Popell
Thank you, Marilyn Reid
Thank you, Michael F Russell
Thank you, Gina Sanfilippo
Thank you, Madeleine Shepherd
Thank you, Michael Stroh
Thank you, Patrick Sullivan
Thank you, Jennifer Waggoner
Thank you, piebob

And a very special thank you to the very modest early subscribers who asked us not to publish their names. You will always have a warm welcome around fire at the Shoreline of Infinity.

We also want to thank those folk who we pestered as we planned and plotted: they provided valuable advice and suggestions. And thanks to those who simply said: "what a great idea!" Every word of encouragement was one pace closer to publication. Thank you especially Steve Green, Duncan Lunan, Mike Calder (Transreal Bookshop), Paul Cockburn, Russell Jones, Dave Alexander, Alan MacGillivray, Tony C. Smith (Starship Sofa), Ren Zelen.

Become a Friend of Shoreline

If you want to join the Friends of Shoreline, please support the magazine by subscribing via our website, www.shorelineofinfinity.com

Our ambition is to pay our writers and artists the full rate for their efforts, and this can only be achieved with the support of our readers.

Remember, for every subscription we receive, a puppy is transformed into a mighty dragon.

www.ingramcontent.com/pod-product-compliance
Ingram Content Group UK Ltd.
Pitfield, Milton Keynes, MK11 3LW, UK
UKHW020135250726
13967UKWH00002B/661

9 780993 441301